TO WORK AND
TO LOVE

TO WORK AND TO LOVE

a theology of creation

Dorothee Soelle
with
Shirley A. Cloyes

FORTRESS PRESS   PHILADELPHIA

Fourth printing 1989

———————————

Library of Congress Cataloging in Publication Data

Soelle, Dorothee.
To work and to love.

"This book originated from a series of lectures entitled 'Creation, work, and sexuality' delivered at Union Theological Seminary in the spring of 1983"— Acknowledgment.
1. Creation. 2. Work (Theology). 3. Sex—Religious aspects—Christianity. 4. Liberation theology.
I. Cloyes, Shirley. II. Title.
BT695.S64 1984   231.7'65   84-47936
ISBN 0–8006–1782–7

———————————

Printed in the United States of America   1-1782

To Jim,
who took me to the home of his boyhood hero at Monticello
and told me that there was nothing wrong
with the pursuit of happiness,
and was a co-creator
before I knew the term co-creation.
To Jim,
who introduced me to the South,
the smell of sweet potatoes and the letters of Bill Faulkner,
who made me shrink and grow
and smiled away my oldest sister, Death,
for a while.
To Jim,
who reconciled me again and again
to the United States of America
and reminded me of its people
when I was scared by its bombs.
To Jim,
who opened my window of vulnerability
and let God's sun shine on us
amid the struggle.
To Jim,
who did all this for me,
and a lot more.

Contents

Acknowledgment

This book originated from a series of lectures entitled "Creation, Work, and Sexuality" delivered at Union Theological Seminary in the spring of 1983. I want to thank my students for listening, questioning, and debating these issues. Using notes, tapes, and additional materials, Shirley Cloyes and I worked on the manuscript. There is not a single line in this book that was not revised, rethought, and reworked by Shirley. The word "with" on the title page indicates much more than editing; it encompasses her correcting my Germanic tongue, clarifying thoughts, rephrasing, struggling over words, often taming the wild flow of associations, and strengthening the argument with her own writing.

Writing about work, we tried to become better workers ourselves, in the sense of being less individualistic. Dreaming of good work, we realized a bit of it. Doing theology in a cooperative way, we moved on to the common language we are in search of. Sisterhood is powerful indeed.

1

Difficulties in praising the God of creation

"And God saw everything that he had made, and behold, it was very good" (Gen. 1:31).[1] This is God's pronouncement on humankind and the rest of creation. It is difficult to agree with God's perspective on creation. Is creation good? Is all of it, everything that God has made, good? Is it "very good"? This book has emerged out of my own struggle to agree with God and to learn to praise creation. Although my own struggle persists, I have come to realize that our capacity to praise 𝒳 creation hinges on our capacity to involve ourselves in creation. No genuine affirmation can arise apart from participation. Only through participation in creation can we affirm it, cherish it, praise it.

For a person to praise something in nature—for instance, a magnolia tree amid the gray monotony of a city street—she has to be involved in that which she extols. Her act of praise means that she has acquired an intimate knowledge of this particular magnolia. She can visualize it in movement or at rest. Its varying hues at different times of the day and night are imprinted on her memory. With her growing sense of this magnolia's beauty comes her own growth. So too the stargazer participates in nature's beauty through naming, recalling, knowing those distant entities, and his praise is nourished through his contemplation of the galaxy. The aesthetic process is the result of our participation in the created order.

When we sing Charles Wesley's hymn "Sing ye heavens, and earth rejoice, Make to God a cheerful noise," we participate in what the heavens are doing. We sing in unison with the heavenly spheres. As we immerse ourselves in the act of singing, we forget ourselves in the union

1

with other voices. Singing in a large group or a choir sometimes engenders the experience of mystical union in which time and space are forgotten and our unanimous "Yes," "Amen," "Hallelujah" temporarily erase the torments of the individual. But these are rare moments of wholeness. Normally, in our day-to-day lives we have no reason to praise God unequivocally. We do not see the magnolia tree or the star; we do not experience unity in song; we do not stand in awe before creation.

If praising the goodness of creation is an act of being alive, then we are dead people most of the time. Is there a life *before* death? This is not a cynical question. We need faith to believe in life before death and to understand that our pain, our injuries, hidden or visible, are neither insurmountable nor automatically death-dealing but finally may lead to a whole life. Too often we do not praise, we do not participate in, we do not believe in a life before death. We frequently witness the death of people before they actually die, a death masquerading as life. It is often far easier for us to trust in the conventional certainty of a life *after* death than in a life of participation in God's ongoing good creation before we die. Choosing life in the face of death means participating in creation through love and work. Sigmund Freud was once asked what a sane, or nonneurotic, person would be like. In reply, he defined the sane person as one who is able to work and to love.

Two factors moved me to write this book now. One, which I share with millions of Europeans and other people currently marching in the streets for peace, is fear. I am afraid of those who plan a "limited" nuclear war and who pave the way for a nuclear holocaust. To reflect on creation today is also to speak of those who wittingly or unwittingly conspire to undo it. On the one hand there is creation and on the other there is "exterminism"—a word coined by British historian Edward P. Thompson to underscore the prevailing disposition of the West to exterminate the biosphere and everything within it.[2] There are three dimensions to exterminism: the rape of the earth, the war against the poor, and the nuclear threat posed by the arms race. Pollution, starvation, and the arms buildup are particular expressions of the death wish that Western societies embrace. As we in the name of "national security" and "getting big government off our backs" stockpile more armaments, make the rich richer, and exhaust more of the earth's unrenewable resources, we must ask ourselves, Are we still in a position to choose creation over exterminism?

When I first heard the phrase "to undo creation," I found myself getting in touch with the depth of my faith in the goodness of creation. It is, I admit, a broken, shaky, often troubled faith. But when I realized that military and political leaders were actually preparing to enact the final solution and the undoing of creation, I knew better than ever before how fathomless my love for creation and "everything God has made" is. It is not just survival instinct that makes me protest and fight against the military machine; I am far more impelled by my unswerving love for creation, and I sense the same love in the hearts of those calling for peace. Those of us who work for peace must know what we are striving for, what kind of life we want to conserve on earth. As the lover knows and remembers the smallest details of the body of her beloved, so too we who love the earth strive to fathom its secrets and to divulge its beauty.

The earth is sacred. Ten years ago I was not so conscious of the sacredness of the earth. It is when we are confronted with the utter threat to that which we love that we rediscover the wellsprings of our love and realize our interdependency anew. The conspiracy to undo creation—or even part of it—in a "winnable" nuclear war reignites our awareness of the sacramentality of the earth, or the earth's nondisposability (*unverfügbarkeit*), to borrow Martin Heidegger's term for existence. The earth is not disposable. Some of its resources are not renewable. We did not create the earth, but we are its stewards. Even if we adopt an atheistic stance, the sacramentality of the earth still lays claims on us, speaking to us and moving us beyond a positivistic world view. There is an often unconscious spirituality at the heart of the peace movement, frequently taking the form of a desperate search for religious reasons and religious discourse that will provide moral foundations for the fight against those who believe they own the earth. When we protest the Pentagon's plans to undo creation, we need to embody a passionate love for creation if we are to counter the despair it manufactures in the form of armaments.[3] And it is for the sake of this passionate love that we also need to reflect theologically on creation.

The other reason I have chosen to write about creation stems from a transformation in my own theological outlook. If asked to explain to a non-Christian why I am still a Christian, I find myself reflecting on three different phases of a religious journey that seem to conform to a larger, Western cultural pattern. The first phase occurs for most of us during our childhood when we are socialized to the religious norms, beliefs, and practices of our ancestors. The religious sensibilities of our ancestors were nourished in small-town or village culture, in which the church was at the center of both social life and spiritual development. Stories and myths, ethics, and values were rooted in and spun around largely unquestioned traditions. Even today, some people will remain all their lives in the religious village. But the majority of us have exited, have moved to the city (if not in actuality, then in our imaginations), and have abandoned prayer and attending church. In the second phase, religion either recedes into oblivion, as it slowly loses whatever powers it once had over people's lives, or becomes the focus of personal exploration, as people seek to assess how their own development has been impaired by their religious socialization and to free themselves from a religion that was imposed on them. A majority of people in this second phase reject their religious heritage and live as post-Christian or post-Jewish inhabitants of the secular city.

But many of us, who cannot live and breathe within the contradictions of the secular city, go in search of sacred ground. Those who enter this third phase consciously choose religion, but not the village version of it. Their choice for religion is postcritical and not naive; it is selective rather than solely receptive. Most people who make this choice after the intense, critical task of phase two are in conflict with their churches and religious communities and will not allow religious authoritarianism to hamstring their lives. Some claim their spirituality only outside the church or synagogue, others rediscover sources of power within their traditions that enable them to struggle against injustice in society and neutrality in religion. Those who move to a critical affirmation of religion strive to develop a new form of lived faith. They do not comprise a back-to-religion trend along the lines of phase one, although many people in phase two harbor that suspicion.

My own religious journey began with phase two. I was born into it. My parents were highly educated members of the German middle class who manifested a certain enlightened condescension towards the church. Challenged by a few Christian friends, but especially by some radical Christian thinkers such as Pascal, Kierkegaard, and Simone Weil, I found myself, as a university student, moving into phase three. My early theological reflection was concerned more with Christ than with God. It was through Christ that I tried again and again to understand God; it was through the brother that I eventually could listen and talk to the father. The second article of the Apostles' Creed was my point of entry; the first was secondary to me. Christ lured me into faith because this human being communicated to me the power of powerless love. My point of departure was the tortured human being from Galilee—Jesus, the worker and the lover, the revolutionary who taught me how to work and to love.

My theological overemphasis on Christ, which I shared with Dietrich Bonhoeffer and others, bypassed the question of God. Like the rest of the theological generation in Europe to which I belong, I was stripped of a naive trust in the Father, Ruler, and Sustainer after two world wars. We fixed our gaze on Christ, the sufferer, because an innocent trust in God was no longer possible. It is not restoration of innocent trust in God that I am after in this book. It may be that I am homesick for God and have been for a long time. Nevertheless, I do not intend to crawl back into the womblike security of some imagined paradise. I do not hanker for the pristine air of a Garden of Eden. But today I find it necessary to ground my early, existentialist *solus Christus* position in a recognition of the source of life itself. Now that God is, for me, no longer imprisoned in images of ruler, king, and father, I want to reconcile my faith in Christ with my new understanding of God the creator. As I move toward a spirituality centered not only in the imitation of Christ but also in creation, I want to spell out what creation means to me and how I participate in it.

Today I sense a need to ground the hope for new life in a new understanding of creation. There may be readers who do not share the specific hope that came to me through a poor Jewish man but who will still accompany me in search of a vision of the created and beloved earth. Dominated by exterminists, we all need to be more aware of the source of our lives and the life of the whole earth. Those who have no sense of the past surely will not have a future. If we want to have a future, then we will need to reclaim our origins. The process of reclaiming our origins will necessarily reveal diverse sources of hope and different saints and fools who at certain points in our lives have connected us with the source of life. Our connection to the source of life is the basis for increased tolerance and unity among us. If we are to thwart the plans of the exterminists, then we must move beyond a concern for religious diversity to concern for religious unity among those who share the earth. To believe in creation is a way to share the earth.

NOTES

1. I have problems with the use of gender-specific nouns for God. At this point in my theological journey, I have decided not to alter the language usage of biblical or theological writers, because I do not want to disguise their biases. In my own theological reflection, my affirmation of God as female seems appropriate, especially when I want to emphatically differentiate my language from that of patriarchal God-talk. She-talk, however, does not by itself sufficiently reveal the scope of the problem of God-talk, nor does it resolve it once and for all. Personalized symbols for God, such as friend, protector, sustainer, or liberator, constitute one mode of God-language, and there are other forms of God-talk equally crucial for expressing our understanding of God. For example, we need the mystical tradition's symbols of God, such as light, fire, depth, life, and voice. The problem of God-talk is not yet solved, because we are in search of "a common language," to echo the poet Adrienne Rich. In an attempt to mirror this search, I have chosen to employ more than one form of God-talk throughout this book.

2. See Edward P. Thompson, "Notes on Exterminism, the Last Stage of Civilization," *New Left Review*, no. 121 (May–June 1980): 3–31.

3. "The 1982 Five-Year Defense Guidance Plan" and "The Pentagon Master Plan," drawn up in the summer of 1982 in response to a White House directive called a "National Security Decision Document," substantiate the shift in U.S. military strategy from deterring to actually fighting a nuclear war. The "National Security Decision Document" is the first U.S. government policy statement to assert that U.S. armed forces must be able to win a protracted nuclear war. "The Pentagon Master Plan" and "The 1982 Five-Year Defense Guidance Plan" outline the military hardware requirements, nuclear targeting adjustments, and general strategy necessary to implement this policy. See Michael Schultheis, "Who Is Misreading Whom?" *Center Focus*, no. 53 (March 1983): 3, 6.

2

In the beginning was liberation

Biblical faith originated from a historical event of liberation, not from belief in creation. For the people of Israel, the Exodus from Egyptian slavery was what Emil L. Fackenheim calls a "root experience" and Severino Croatto calls a "radical datum."[1] The Exodus event is radical in the literal sense of the word that is derived from the Latin *radix*, meaning root, and in the wider political sense that we use the word today to characterize those who work for freedom. A root experience is a public, historical event that, although not undergone firsthand, continues to have the utmost relevance for later generations who have chosen to stand in the same tradition.

The roots of a tree are alive in its branches and trunk; without its roots, the tree would be lifeless. The metaphor of the root evokes the relation between the past and the present that makes a past event "legislative to the present."[2] To return to the roots of the Jewish and Christian traditions means to understand the historical project of liberation carried out in the Exodus, before moving on to the ontological project that God inaugurated in the creation of the universe. Both projects, the historical and the ontological, are aimed at the freedom of the human being, and both projects need human agency—which is one of the claims of this book.

In a famous essay written in 1936, Gerhard von Rad argues that Israel's enduring faith was the result of Yahweh's primary redemptive deeds.[3] In his opinion, faith in creation was a comparatively late development and decidedly an ancillary and secondary belief. He cites the composition of the Book of Exodus prior to Genesis as evidence for the earlier ascendancy of liberation faith. But more significant for von Rad is the textual evidence that Israel's concept of God grew out of the historical deed of God's deliverance of the Hebrew people. That God acted with liberating power on behalf of God's chosen people in a specific historical time and space and under particular circumstances was the decisive factor in the Israelite understanding of God and humanity.

It is in light of the Hebrews' being freed from oppression by a foreign military superpower that we have to approach the conceptualization of creation in the biblical narratives of Genesis 1 and 2. The Exodus event precedes Jewish faith in creation and its exposition in narrative form. In the words of Croatto, "Genesis is an 'interpretation' of Exodus, expressed in the language of the origins, of the ontological 'project' of human beings."[4] To speak of the ontological project is to address the essential meaning of human life in the world, beginning with the fact that we were created for freedom. But the only way to understand the ontological project is to grasp the historical project of humankind. If Genesis interprets Exodus, then the ontological project of our very being serves the historical project of our becoming free.

The Exodus event left its indelible mark on the memory of the cult, which in turn embodied the event in its religious institutions: "You shall remember that you were a slave in Egypt" (Deut. 16:12a). The cult did not have a purely ritualistic function; it created historical consciousness of Israel's freedom. Even the Sabbath, a central institution in Jewish life which is often understood to commemorate God's respite after six days of creating the universe, is related to Israel's liberation from Egyptian bondage in the imagination of the Deuteronomist:

> You shall remember that you were a servant in the land of Egypt, and the Lord your God brought you out thence with a mighty hand and an outstretched arm; therefore the Lord your God commanded you to keep the sabbath day. (Deut. 5:15)

If liberation precedes creation, then soteriology precedes cosmology. An old confession of faith underscores this theological orientation in ancient Israel:

> And you shall make response before the Lord your God. A wandering Aramean was my father; and he went down into Egypt and sojourned there, few in number; and there he became a nation, great, mighty, and popu-

lous. And the Egyptians treated us harshly, and afflicted us, and laid upon us hard bondage. Then we cried to the Lord the God of our fathers, and the Lord heard our voice, and saw our affliction, our toil, and our oppression; and the Lord brought us out of Egypt with a mighty hand and an outstretched arm, with great terror, with signs and wonders; and he brought us into this place and gave us this land, a land flowing with milk and honey. (Deut. 26:5–9)

The emphasis in the preceding passage is again on liberation. The "wandering Aramean," a landless and homeless person, was not consoled by the starry skies above him. It was rather the historical action of a God who liberates that established his identity and made him feel at home in a new land. The passage teaches how to "make response before the Lord your God." To respond to God implies that God has already talked to you through God's action of freeing the enslaved. The passage describes a dialogue between a people and their God. Memory, then, becomes the indispensable companion of faith, and forgetfulness is sin because it implies a lack of response to God's action in history. To remember is a categorical imperative in Judaism, and one that through Judaism applies to all of us. We must *remember* if we want to be in touch with the source of life. It is not creation that grants us our freedom; rather, we are enabled to understand creation in light of our memory and experience of liberation.

It is not necessary to interpret the liberation tradition as exclusive to Judaism over against other religious or secular traditions. The Jewish tradition reveals to the human family that we are created for freedom and that freedom is our historical project. Judaism talks to us in the powerful language of the Exodus tradition about a God who wills freedom for the oppressed and affirms the Liberator as the Creator. There are other "root experiences" in other peoples' histories, such as Christ's resurrection from the dead and Gandhi's march to the Indian Ocean. My intent is not to exclude other liberation traditions, but to understand the link between the two religious concepts of liberation and creation as they come together in Judaism.

There is a theological debate over the strict delineation of creation traditions versus liberation traditions. George Landes, for example, argues that the separation of cosmic creation faith from liberation faith is wrong.[5] He states that even in the Exodus tradition the forces and elements of nature, as well as human agents, play an important role. The plagues, the Red Sea, the wind, and other natural elements are harnessed to oppose the Egyptians by the only one who could harness them: the Creator. Landes tries to bring both creation and liberation traditions together, as the biblical tradition does. But like many conservative biblical scholars, he fails to understand the liberation argument, namely, that we need liberation before we can affirm creation. At the very least, oppressed people need a God who sides with them against the oppressor. The cosmic order as such, without a liberation tradition, does not reconcile slaves and other oppressed peoples, because it cannot empower them to free themselves.

Creation faith is susceptible to the danger of "cheap reconciliation," whereby we are asked to live as if we did not require freeing from present, unjust orders, as if the presumption of a universal transhistorical order were sufficient in itself for human life, and as if the God of nature had triumphed over the God of history. The oppressed have an epistemological advantage: They wait for a greater God. Creation is not yet finished. Both projects, the historical and the ontological, are aimed at the freedom of the human being, and it is one of the claims of this book that both projects need human agency. Participation in the ontological project of creation—human liberation—is possible only for the Exodus people, who have experienced at least once the liberating empowerment of the source of life. The universal source of life is not endlessly available to us, but, as the Jewish and Christian traditions claim, comes to us through particular historical events.

Today's creationists present a case for a literal belief in God's work of

THE CREATION TRADITION VERSUS THE LIBERATION TRADITION	
Creation Tradition	*Liberation Tradition*
Creation	Liberation
Prehistory	History
Universal	Particular
Humanity's tradition	Israel's salvation

six days and manifest spiritual blindness to the liberation tradition of the Bible. Theirs is an objectively cynical system bereft of the two great strengths of faith: memory and hope. The words "You shall remember ✗ that you were a slave in Egypt" are forgotten by creationists, who sever creation faith from its liberation context. They uproot the concept of creation from its biblical *Sitz im Leben* (milieu), that is, the liberation event of the people of Israel. When there is no memory of liberation, ✗ there can be no hope. Turning its back on liberation, creationism dehistoricizes what creation faith really is and reveals nothing of substantial relevance for people's lives. For creationists, objectively speaking, the whole world has become the Egypt of the oppressor in which even the need for liberation is destroyed. The failure to reveal the truth of creation and its ontological project is matched, in creationism, by the attempt to control people's lives and thoughts and to weaken their self-determination.

As I stated above, my attempt in this book is to interpret creation faith in light of liberation theology and the ontological project in light of the historical project. We need to achieve a synthesis of creation and liberation traditions that does not devalue the liberation tradition but rather apprehends the creation tradition from a liberation perspective. The biblical affirmation "Our help is in the name of the Lord, who made heaven and earth" (Ps. 124:8) takes liberation, here simply called "help," as our starting point, the experience from which we move forward into a recognition of God's good creation. In the beginning was liberation; it is in terms of this beginning that we approach the dimensions of our createdness.

Let us now turn to the Priestly account of creation (Gen. 1:1 — 2:4a), ✗ a story that runs counter to the culture and religion of the Babylonians. It was over against Babylonian religious beliefs and their mythologizing of the cosmic-political powers that Israel defined its understanding of creation, nature, and the role of the human being. During their exile, the Israelites had become acquainted with the world view of the superpower of Babylon. They had sojourned in the court of the king to whom all people, regardless of race and nationality, were expected to be subservient. According to the Sumerian-Babylonian creation myth, in the beginning of the world there was inordinate chaos while many gods fought and vied for power. Eventually the strongest god subdued the others and became the king. The vanquished gods were pressed into the king's service as his court and stripped of their independence. As time went by, these lesser deities became enervated by the increasing demands of this "sacred" king. They convened to resolve the problem and ultimately decided to create a servant for themselves. This servant was the first human being.[6]

The Babylonian creation myth was a prescription for social inequality: the king was God's representative on earth; the palace elites enjoyed the wealth and power of life at court; the mass of people labored. The Babylonian creation myth, which celebrated the creation of the human being as the liberation of the gods from the yoke of labor, served to reinforce a hierarchical social system in the context of the cult. From the earliest Sumerian times, large economic enterprises were connected to the temple and its cult. The mass of common people labored for the cult, erecting its temples and palaces and producing food. Their lot was to serve the king, the priests, the administrators, and the gods above them. Unlike the Babylonian myth's emphasis on human subjugation, the biblical narrative portrays the human being as lord over the rest of creation and "made in the image of God." Although the great religious traditions of Egypt and Mesopotamia also understood the human being as made in the image of some god, various Oriental texts reveal that this privilege was reserved for the king or the Pharaoh.

In Babylonian religion the study of the stars played a pivotal role. Astronomy, in this context, was the sole province of the educated, ruling elites, whereas astrology was the religious vehicle of the masses. Members of the court had their own stars, which they required people to venerate. The stars, ranked in importance according to size, were on the one hand religious symbols of the power of the court and on the other hand representations of various deities. To the Babylonians the stars were sky gods.[7] By contrast, the biblical narrative in Genesis 1 refers to the stars as the work of a greater God who hung them in the sky as lamps to give light to the earth and to separate day and night. God made the stars for the people who inhabit the earth below; according to the Bible, they are useful instruments not astral deities. God and the world are distinct in the biblical tradition. The message that comes out of the Priestly account of creation in Genesis is that God is not to be identified with the world.

Christianity adopted the Israelite version of creation, in which God is distinct from the world and human beings are not set in hierarchical relation to one another. It is precisely at this juncture, however, where Christianity emphasized the distinctiveness and separateness of God from the world and humanity from the earth, that our scrutiny and questioning of the Christian tradition must begin. When I try to express faith in creation in light of liberation theology, the question then becomes: Which elements in creation faith and creation thought are liberating and which are oppressive? It is liberating to know that there is no domination over human beings by human beings prescribed or implied in the Old Testament creation myth. The biblical myth cannot be used to legitimate either state power, racism, or sexism, even though it has traditionally functioned as a rationale for patriarchal sexism, especially by virtue of the Yahwist's account in Gen. 2:4b—3:24.[8] There are, nevertheless, other pitfalls in the Christian tradition, of which one of the most harmful is the emphasis on the distinctive and separate character of the Godhead over against the world. In contrast to this emphasis in Christianity, a different creation myth, as articulated by Sakokwenonkwas, a Native American subchief of the Mohawk nation, stresses unity between God and the creation:

> We believe that when the Mystery, or God, created the universe, he placed his hand on the whole thing, so everything is spiritual. As far as I know, God never told us Mohawks to separate anything, but just to look upon everything that he made as holy and sacred and act accordingly with respect.[9]

Western theology, however, has stressed God's separateness from creation in order to elevate God's absolute transcendence. In interpreting the concept of creation, the overriding tendency of the orthodox theological tradition—in opposition to heretical and mystical countercurrents—has been to remove God from creation, to emphasize God's wholly other status, to see him as the absolutely transcendent Lord.

There is the seed of separation between God and the world in Genesis and throughout the Pentateuch, because these stories were written in part to demonstrate Yahweh's superiority over Baal, Astarte, Marduk, and other nature gods. God's being *in* the world, of which there is ample evidence throughout the Old Testament, was played down in the creation account in rejection of the flagrant pantheistic aspects of foreign cult worship. But Christianity, and especially orthodox theology, furthered the bias against pantheism, finally separating God from the world entirely. Pantheism rapidly became a heresy in Christianity. God as the unique source of all life was equated with the God who created out of nothingness. Separateness, as a quality of divinity, became extolled as a virtue in and of itself. The independence of God was understood as intrinsic to divinity, and unrelatedness was considered a sign of God's greatness and glory.

The theological presumption of God's absolute otherness has consequences in three dimensions: for God, for the earth, and for the human being. If God is absolutely transcendent, then God is rendered invisible as the Creator for whom there can be no human analogies. There is no interaction beween such a creator and us. He creates the world out of his free will; he does not need to create it. His creation is an act of absolute freedom. Absolute transcendence literally means unrelatedness. Classical theology viewed the opposite of unrelatedness—relationality—as the weakness of a being bound through passion and suffering to other beings. Hence, the transcendent God in his absolute freedom is a projection of the patriarchal world view and its ideal of the independent king, warrior, or hero.

In the opposite vein, the black poet and activist James Weldon Johnson envisioned God as a needy being who created the world out of loneliness. He offers us a different version of the creation story:

And God stepped out on space,
And he looked around and said:
I'm lonely—
I'll make me a world.[10]

God's loneliness and God's need for the other is the beginning of creation. It makes no sense to postulate God's absoluteness, because then the fact of creation becomes nothing more than an arbitrary decision. The theological overemphasis on God's freedom to create or not to create mirrors the desire of orthodox male theologians to transcend interdependency, to enter a realm of imaginary, absolute freedom beyond relatedness, beyond love, and beyond justice. But who needs such a God? Surely not the black writer of this poem on creation.

Johnson's poem diverges from the predominant theological tradition in another significant way. The Priestly account in Genesis 1 depicts God's work as the result of God's words. God proclaims, "Let there be light," and light appears. God does not work with his hands like a craftsman or artist. Instead, God orders creation into being. God's instrument is the authority and power of the divine word. Johnson, however, portrays God's work of creation differently:

> And far as the eye of God could see
> Darkness covered everything,
> Blacker than a hundred midnights
> Down in a cypress swamp.
>
> Then God smiled,
> And the light broke,
> And the darkness rolled up on one side,
> And the light stood shining on the other,
> And God said: That's good!
>
> Then God reached out and took the light in his hands,
> And God rolled the light around in his hands
> Until he made the sun;
> And he set that sun a-blazing in the heavens.[11]

The God in this narrative poem works physically. God uses a smile, hands, and feet to do the work of creation. All that remains of his almighty words in this version of the creation story is the folksy refrain "That's good!" with which God greets each new facet of the universe.

Johnson interweaves the disparate elements of the Yahwist and Priestly accounts of creation. He uses the format and sequence of the narrative in Genesis 1 and the anthropomorphist portrayal of God working manually in the Yahwist's account in Genesis 2. The implicit theology of the poem is one of mutuality, interdependence, and motherliness, as opposed to a theology of authoritative power, independence, and absolute freedom. The poem continues:

> Then God walked around,
> And God looked around
> On all that he had made.
> He looked at his sun,
> And he looked at his moon,
> And he looked at his little stars;

He looked on his world
With all its living things,
And God said: I'm lonely still.

Then God sat down—
On the side of a hill where he could think;
By a deep, wide river he sat down;
With his head in his hands,
God thought and thought,
Till he thought: I'll make me a man![12]

This God needs the other. Relatedness is inseparable from this God
who is able to experience loneliness.

Love needs the presence and involvement of another being; love cannot exist without the other. Self-sufficiency is a concept of the lonely
and unrelated person. To conceive of creation in the framework of unrelatedness is to deprive creation of its most central element—love.
Whatever meaning we find in the concept of creation, in a creator, and
in our having been created hinges on love. The concept of creation is
rendered empty and meaningless if it is not out of love that God created
the world.

We need to understand ourselves as having been expected and cherished before we came into the world. A child who grows up with a
profound sense of being unwanted and not needed by her parents rarely
develops basic trust in herself. Conversely, a child secure in her parents'
love will trust herself to the point of projecting her own being back-
ward in time, asking, "What did you do before I was born? Didn't you
miss me?" Our sense of self-worth and dignity is rooted in our being
needed, if not by our parents then by someone else who values who we
are. The religious expression of the fundamental human desire to be
needed is found in our creation myths, which tell us that God waited
for us and that God needs us.

The second consequence stemming from God's otherness is related
to our understanding of the earth. The concept of reality developed by
modern scientists dismissed the theological understanding of creation.
The wholly otherness of God has served as theology's escape valve away
from dialogue with the scientific community. Theology, in effect, has
left the natural world to the scientists. Science, meanwhile, has tended
to ignore the relation of reality and the *res extensae* to creation, and most
Christians have viewed faith in creation as an absorption in the mere

factuality or "thatness" of the universe. Emptied of substance, this kind of faith in creation has lost sight of what it means to affirm a created universe.

God's wholly otherness makes the world into a godless place. Insofar as God is wholly other, there can be no sanctity, no divine reality in the world. The world is reduced to matter and fact. There is no basis for awe and wonder if divine reality is totally external to and independent from the world. A positivistic world view is contagious; it infects even those who have a stake in a God removed in time and space. Transcendence without immanence becomes reified, and then it cannot touch or affect us. As the theological concept of creation is reduced to the mere positing of the creation of the world by God, devoid of all sacramental feeling, the spirituality of creation, thus unhinged from immanence, simply dries up.

One of the consummate speeches of the nineteenth century is the address of the Squamish Chief Seattle to the "Great Chief" in Washington, D.C. This speech, which integrates politics and religion, was delivered in 1854 to mark the transferral of ancestral Indian lands to the federal government:

> How can you buy or sell the sky, the warmth of the land? The idea is strange to us. . . .
>
> Every part of this earth is sacred to my people. Every shining pine needle, every sandy shore, every mist in the dark woods, every clearing and humming insect is holy in the memory and experience of my people. The sap which courses through the trees carries the memories of the red man. . . .
>
> This shining water that moves in the streams and rivers is not just water but the blood of our ancestors. If we sell you land, you must remember that it is sacred, and you must teach your children that it is sacred, and that each ghostly reflection in the clear water of the lake tells of events and memories in the life of my people. The water's murmur is the voice of my father's father.
>
> The rivers are our brothers, they quench our thirst. The rivers carry our canoes, and feed our children. If we sell you our land, you must remember, and teach your children, that the rivers are our brothers, and yours, and you must henceforth give the rivers the kindness you would give my brother.
>
> The red man has always retreated before the advancing white man, as the mist of the mountain runs before the morning sun. But the ashes of our fathers are sacred. Their graves are holy ground, and so these hills, these trees, this portion of earth is consecrated to us. We know that the

white man does not understand our ways. One portion of land is the same to him as the next, for he is a stranger who comes in the night and takes from the land whatever he needs. The earth is not his brother, but his enemy, and when he has conquered it, he moves on. He leaves his fathers' graves behind, and he does not care. He kidnaps the earth from his children. He does not care. His fathers' graves and his children's birthright are forgotten. He treats his mother, the earth, and his brother, the sky, as things to be bought, plundered, sold like sheep or bright beads. His appetite will devour the earth and leave behind only a desert.[13]

This red man's eloquent testimony to the sacredness of the earth ends in a stark assessment of the white man's perfidies and his potential to destroy nature. The attitude of the Native American toward the earth is rooted in a profound sense of relatedness based on our oneness with nature. For this Native American, God exists within the created world and is not absolute ruler and lord over it. Consequently, the earth is not just matter that we may exploit with impunity. To believe in creation from the perspective of a religious tradition that retains close ties to nature would mean to affirm the sacredness of all life on earth, not just our own. Our imperialistic stance toward nature has deep roots in our overly transcendental, monotheistic, and patriarchal religious tradition. The liberating elements in the Christian orthodox doctrine of creation are counterposed by its oppressive elements. One of the oldest objects of oppression and exploitation is the earth.

To rediscover and reimage the liberating parts of our religious heritage is one of the most urgent tasks for theology today. Those who work creatively on this renaming of God are those who are hurt most by the oppressive parts of the Christian tradition. Feminist religious groups are in the vanguard of this venture, creating over the last decade the most exquisite, moving, and daring forms of new liturgy. A liturgical poem by Carter Heyward reads:

In the beginning was God
In the beginning
the source of all that is
In the beginning
God yearning

God moaning
God laboring
God giving birth

God rejoicing
And God loved what she had made.
And God said,
"It is good."

And God, knowing that all that is good is shared
held the earth tenderly in her arms.
God yearned for relationship.
God longed to share the good earth,
And humanity was born in the yearning of God
We were born to share the earth.[14]

This liturgical poem is feminist, not just because it is written by a female theologian and refers to God as she but also because of the author's perspective on creation, in which God and the human being share the earth together, visible in the imagery of an earthly mother and a God as dependent as love is.

The third consequence of Western belief in an absolutely transcendent God concerns the role of the human being. The biblical creation myth accentuates the domination of the human being over the earth. Humans are depicted in Genesis as different from other animals and from nature. The distinctiveness of the human being in comparison with our natural siblings, plants and animals, is overstated. The upshot of this strident distinction is that we have lost the awareness of and reverence for what we share with nonhuman living things. We are as dependent as they are on air, water, light, and food. We are as disposed to frailty and death, but our imperialism against nature makes us forget and suppress our common fate. Chief Seattle reminds us of our shared destiny:

The air is precious to the red man, for all things share the same breath— the beast, the tree, the man, they all share the same breath. The white man does not seem to notice the air he breathes. Like a man dying for many days, he is numb to the stench. But if we sell you our land, you must remember that the air is precious to us, that the air shares its spirit with all the life it supports. The wind that gave our grandfather his first breath also receives his last sigh. And the wind must also give our children the spirit of life. And if we sell you our land, you must keep it apart and sacred, as a place where even the white man can go to taste the wind that is sweetened by the meadow's flowers.

So we will consider your offer to buy our land. If we decide to accept, I will make one condition: The white man must treat the beasts of this land as his brothers.

I am a savage and do not understand any other way. I have seen a thousand rotting buffaloes on the prairie, left by the white man who shot them from a passing train. I am a savage and I do not understand how the smoking iron horse can be more important than the buffalo that we kill only to stay alive. What is man without the beasts? If all the beasts were gone, men would die from a great loneliness of spirit. For whatever happens to the beasts, soon happens to man. All things are connected. . . . This we know. The earth does not belong to man: man belongs to the earth. This we know. All things are connected like the blood which unites one family. All things are connected.[15]

If we were to grasp the connectedness of all living things, we might recover a humble spirit in the face of creation. God's otherness as a theological concept makes us strangers on earth. Otherness is the prerequisite for domination and the will to power.

The three oppressive consequences of the classical Christian doctrine of creation are (1) the total otherness of God and God's domination over men, women, animals, and the earth; (2) a godless matter-of-fact earth; and (3) human loneliness, presumed to be the a priori, incontrovertible essence of the human condition. The ecological catastrophe that now envelops us has its roots, in part, in Christian tradition. If we would develop a new understanding of creation, we need a critical awareness of the destructiveness of our faith. The distinction between oppressive and liberating elements in all our theologies and traditions has to be clarified again and again. A theology of creation must teach us how to love the earth better.

NOTES

1. See Emil L. Fackenheim, *God's Presence in History: Jewish Affirmations and Philosophical Reflections* (New York: Harper & Row, 1970), p. 9; and J. Severino Croatto, *Exodus: A Hermeneutics of Freedom*, trans. Salvator Attanasio (Maryknoll, N.Y.: Orbis Books, 1981), p. 13.

2. Fackenheim, *God's Presence in History*, p. 9.

3. Gerhard von Rad, "Das theologische Problem des alttestamentlichen Schöpfungsglaubens," in *Werden und wesen des Alten Testaments*, Beiheft 66 zur *Zeitschrift für die alttestamentliche Wissenschaft* (1936): 138–147.

4. Croatto, *Exodus*, p. 31.

5. George M. Landes, "Creation and Liberation," *Union Seminary Quarterly Review* 33, no. 2 (Winter 1978): 79–89.

6. Claus Westermann, *Schöpfung* (Berlin: Kreuz-Verlag Stuttgart, 1971), pp. 73ff.

7. Ibid., p. 64.

8. See Phyllis Trible, *God and the Rhetoric of Sexuality* (Philadelphia: Fortress Press, 1978), p. 18.

9. Sakokwenonkwas, "The Road Back to Our Future," *Gamaliel* 3, no. 1 (Spring 1977): 35.

10. James Weldon Johnson, "The Creation," in *God's Trombones: Seven Negro Sermons in Verse* (New York: Penguin Books, 1981; reprint of the 1969 edition), p. 17.

11. Ibid., pp. 17–18.

12. Ibid., pp. 19–20.

13. "The Unforked Message of Chief Seattle," in *Flesh and Spirit: A Religious View of Bicentennial America, Gamaliel* (Washington, D.C.: Community for Creative Nonviolence, 1976), p. 72.

14. A selection from Carter Heyward, "Blessing the Bread: A Litany" in *Our Passion for Justice: Images of Power, Sexuality, and Liberation* (New York: Pilgrim Press, 1984).

15. "The Unforked Message of Chief Seattle," p. 73.

3

Made
from dust

The goal of a creation theology is to empower us to say "Yes!" "Indeed!" "Amen!" "It *is* very good." But it is difficult to reach the point where we can praise creation. Our experience of reality does not lead us to acclaim the goodness of creation. There is no natural way to affirm creation, but there is a basic need, even in those of us who suffer extreme deprivation and hardship, to affirm creation. Faith is the fruit of struggle with doubt and despair. That is why it is so hard to utter a genuine, not a cheap, "Hallelujah." Is there a theology that can bolster our faith in creation? Theology should offer a rational support system that clarifies our thought and sustains our belief in the face of doubt and despair. But the traditional theological concept of creation does not do what it should. It does not help me to praise the God of creation, because it portrays that God as Lord and Maker at the cost of my very being.

Our difficulty in praising creation stems from the traditional split in our understanding between God as the Lord, the subject of creation, and the human being as the object, or the "stuff" of creation made from dust.

Is it true that the Bible talks about an infinite gap between the Creator and the created? Is it not true that this dichotomy instead represents what our tradition has chosen to select from the Bible? We have to ask ourselves a basic question: If we locate God at one end of the spectrum as the creator and the world at the other end as the created, where is the human being? Are we objects? Are we, for instance, inanimate clay pots in the hands of the Potter? Does the allegory of the potter in

---

THE TRADITIONAL DISTINCTION BETWEEN
GOD AND THE WORLD

God	*The World*
Creator	Created
Lord	Servant
Maker	Made
Artist	Artifact
Will or form	Stuff or matter
Cause	Effect
Subject	Object

Jer. 18:1–12 describe who we are? Can we understand ourselves in this way? Nothing will assuage my anger about the way this image has been used in the Christian tradition to humiliate the human being, to cut us off from our freedom, to dismiss us as "stuff," as some sort of dead material. What I object to most fiercely is that the Christian tradition gives all the power to the Potter while debasing the pot.

The problem with the supposedly unbridgeable gap between the creator and the created is that it has been transposed, for example, into sexist dichotomizing, in which we ascribe "godly" characteristics to the male and "worldly" characteristics to the female. The ontological concept is used in a sexist sense. Indeed, many injurious dichotomies flow out of our positing an unequivocal separation between God and humanity. Must we subscribe to this imperialistic concept of creation? Is there not a different way of construing creation and the relationship between God and the world? I believe that we need to reconceive the divine-human relationship, the doctrine of creation-out-of-nothingness (because it enhances the dichotomy traditionally posed between the creator and the created), and the notion of the absolute, autocratic freedom of the creator. The whole structure of domination that the orthodox concept of God reflects is captured in the Latin word for lord, *dominus*. *Dominus*, as well as the Greek *kyrios*, is the coercive, feudal ruler. The image of a God who rules over his subjects lends itself to sustaining worldly forms of oppression and exploitation. Again, is there a nonimperialistic concept of creation that posits an alternative understanding of the relation between God and the world? Process theology represents one attempt in the West to articulate a different understanding of the divine-human relationship. In Alfred North Whitehead's philosophy and that of his followers (most notably Charles Hartshorne), "becoming," not "being," is the fundamental, ontological category. From a process perspective, everything that lives, moves, and grows constitutes a process, not a substance. And God is not exempt from this dynamic ontology. Process thought thereby offers a corrective to classical Western philosophy's elevation of "being" as the ultimate and most significant category for creation. It challenges classical philosophy's corollary assumption that reality consists of unchangeable substances which entertain only accidental relationships. It transforms the classical concept of God *a se*, to use a scholastic term, a God "in himself" who engages in relationships at whim.

In contrast to the concept of God *a se*, process thought considers relationship a necessary ingredient in any understanding of what we would call God. Relationship, then, is essential for God; it is not something that incidentally enters into the picture. "In the beginning is the relation," Martin Buber tells us in *I and Thou*.[1] Process thought shares with Buber the belief that just as relationship is not accidental to God, so too the world is not accidental. Reality consists of interrelated processes, events, and occasions of experience. God's absoluteness is relativized by this concept.

Process thought depicts reality in bipolar terms: potentiality and actuality, change and permanence, relativity and absoluteness, becoming and being. In Whitehead's framework, if God was alone before creation, there was the potentiality in God to create the world, but it was not yet actualized. Likewise, there is permanence in God, but this permanence consists of God's ability to change, to express herself in a variety of ways, and to reveal herself in different forms. There is a beautiful phrase in process theology which says that God is "the self-surpassing surpasser of all."[2] In other words, God surpasses God; God is always greater than God is at any given moment because of God's potentiality. And God's potential cannot be actualized if God does not change, if God is *a se*—hence the significance of the process principle that every

action is an interaction. There is no action either by God or by humanity that exists "in itself," or *a se*. God is permanent or unchangeable in
that God continually offers new possibilities. In other words, God loves
us always. Both God's unchangeability and the fact that God will always
surpass God are affirmed by God's renewed offerings of love. God's
constancy is love, but God's permanence is not static. Similarly, God
foresees our possibilities, but does not know which ones we shall
choose. God knows our potentiality but awaits its actualization, leaving
space for our freedom.

It is through interaction that God's love is revealed, and in process
theology it is through interaction that the world becomes the body of
God. Each organism touches and changes the organism that influences
it. Likewise, we act on God, and God receives things from us. Process
theologians adopt a unified perspective in which God does not reside in
a "second world" above history, but on the contrary lives in and
through history as we do.

Although from another perspective it would be easy to launch a full-
scale criticism of process thought as an exclusively philosophical
outlook unconcerned with sociopolitical realities in a world of human
suffering, this is not my intention here. Instead I have stressed those aspects of process thought that contribute to our overcoming the imperialism inherent in traditional theology's concept of the divine-human
relation.

Religious feminists offer other insights and approaches to overcoming the split in traditional theology between the creator and the created.
The work of feminist theologian Carter Heyward is a case in point.
Heyward affirms a divine-human relation that is "reciprocal, dynamic,
and of benefit to both parties."[3] Defining God as our "power in relation to each other, all humanity, and creation itself,"[4] she asks us to
"take seriously the creative character of who we are—both in relation
to one another (humanity) and to the power of relation itself (God.)"[5]
According to her, this is our vocation. The language that Heyward
employs in *The Redemption of God: A Theology of Mutual Relation* is a
language of freedom which itself conveys a liberating power. Her horizon is freedom; liberation from subjection is her concern. She seeks to
overcome the traditional theological split between the creator and the
created by affirming the relatedness of all things and our co-creative

partnership with God in doing the work of love and justice. She objects to the classical and neo-orthodox tendency to give disproportionate importance to the divine, arguing that neo-orthodoxy, in particular, "provides a paradigm for the legitimation of an 'over-and-against' relation, in which the higher possesses a Truth with which it penetrates the lower, who receives it with great thanksgiving."[6]

The distinction that Heyward draws between authority (*exousia*) and power (*dynamis*) is crucial to our surmounting the notion that all the power belongs to the "wholly other." In her schema, *exousia* is the "socially licensed" power of the one over the other, the kind of power we associate with religious and civil government, whereas the power that she calls *dynamis* is a "spontaneous," "raw," "self-attributed," "unlicensed" power, inviting and luring us into itself.[7] Reminiscent of the concept of power in process thought, *dynamis* is mutual, reciprocal, shared power. Heyward's distinction between *exousia* and *dynamis* is equivalent to a distinction between good power and evil power. The powerful person needs to share his or her power with others. Only shared power is good power. Real power is not something that *someone* owns. Evil power in the service of domination, whether by God or humanity, is another matter.

In addition to process thought and feminist theology, there is another basis for rethinking the concept of creation in philosophical materialism. Orthodox Christian theology has embraced idealism and rejected philosophical materialism. The idealist philosophical framework emphasizes the ruling power of the mind over subjected matter. By contrast, philosophical materialism takes matter seriously. In Europe there is discussion about a new approach to biblical exegesis from the perspective of philosophical materialism. Unlike an exegetical approach based on idealism, this reading of the Bible takes the body and society seriously. This not only signals a new development inside the exegetical tradition but also marks a shift in the philosophical, or systematic theological, question. From the perspective of philosophical materialism, reality is matter in motion, and we do not need other principles in order to explain it. Philosophical materialists are not bent on proclaiming the doctrine that everything in the world, including thought, will, and feeling, can be explained undialectically in terms of matter. They are motivated by the attempt to understand matter, "stuff," or the reality of the body in its living motion and process and to apprehend its creative power. My own effort to interpret creation in light of such earthly things as work and sexuality is an example of a materialistic philosophical approach. Mine is a poetic materialism that affirms sensuousness and beauty as they are transmitted through the living, moving material, or "stuff," of this world.

The theological term "incarnation" expresses the earthiness, the materialistic fabric, of our being in God. It is important for us to understand the spirit as incarnate in the body. We are embodied, living entities. The significance of this notion for our self-understanding is well illustrated by the presence of two words for the body in the German language. One is *Leib*, which is equivalent to "life" in English. The other German word for the body is *Körper*, which corresponds to the English "corpse." *Leib* is related to life, whereas *Körper* is the machine-like, dead thing. My body as *Leib* is a living entity. As *Körper*, it has the quality of a dead thing that can be controlled, ruled, dominated. To speak of my body as *Leib* is to speak of my very being. I *am* my body. I don't *have* a body; I don't *own* my body. My body is who I am, whereas the *Körper* is something that can be possessed. Only the *Körper* belongs to the order of having; *Leib* belongs to the order of being.

My preceding remarks about philosophical materialism and the body are intended as a prologue to presenting an embodied theology, which I would like to develop by means of three maxims. The first maxim is "I am made from dust." The second maxim is a quotation from the 1854 speech of the Native American Chief Seattle: "The earth does not belong to the human being, but the human being belongs to the earth." The third maxim is "The earth is the Lord's" (Ps. 24:1) or "La tierra es al Señor," as voiced by the *campesinos* in many past and present Latin American peasant revolts.

What does our being made from dust mean? My free associations form a kind of meditation:

> I am limited in time, in space, in strength, in power;
> I am frail, perishable, decaying;
> I am bound by biology;
> I have only limited choices, choices conditioned by my life in the body . . .

For example, I menstruate. It is a fact of my life as a woman. Menstruation is not something I can overcome or extinguish, nor would I wish to. To do so would require my killing something in myself—destroying something intrinsic to my very being. My choices are limited by virtue of my being made from dust. And the theological question that ensues is: Can I affirm myself as one who is made from dust? Can I say that my having been created is very good? How do I, as a person made from dust, respond to the ontological project of being created for freedom? To pose the question another way, is it possible for me to say that all things are "very good" because of their origins in God? Is it possible for me to value my "creatureliness" in the knowledge that my existence was willed prior to my birth, that I am not here on this earth simply by chance, that I am needed, that I am not a disposable object, and that I am designed for freedom and equality?

We are born into an ontological project that has been entrusted to the human race from the beginning; we experience this as the historical project of liberation. As human beings, we are born into the process of liberation. If we fail to take this project seriously, we miss our vocation. We are created in God's image, and yet we are made from dust. If we are to affirm our createdness, we can deny neither our frailty, earthiness, and mortality nor the ontological project of liberation that God has in mind for all of us. That we are willed, needed, projected, and formed by God is the greatest affirmation we can bring to our lives. This kind of self-affirmation is the result of our having been created. Yet we are made from dust. The tension between these two poles of our self-understanding seems irreconcilable until we realize that affirming our createdness means embracing both sides of the dialectic.

Again, what does it mean to be made from dust? Being made from dust reminds me of being in and with the body. The history of Christianity has been marked by a rejection of the principal dimensions of this "dust factor." This "dust factor" accounts for the body and the society. My body tells me that I am in pain, hungry, have sexual needs. It is through my body that I know that it is not so very good here on earth. The wrong way to relieve this tension is to deny and to suppress the body and its needs in favor of affirming an idealistic spirituality cleansed of all bodily desires. An idealistic spirituality is the enemy of a creational spirituality. It is based on the dualism of self and body, or the body-spirit dichotomy that we inherited from Greek philosophy. Socrates, as transmitted by Plato in the *Phaedo*, says:

> It seems that so long as we are alive, we shall continue closest to knowledge if we avoid as much as we can all contact and association with the body, except when they are absolutely necessary; and instead of allowing ourselves to become infected with its nature, purify ourselves from it until God himself gives us deliverance.[8]

Most of us know the feeling of being ashamed of our body, the wish to extricate ourselves from our body, even the hate of our body. Sometimes the soul is a stranger to the body and longs to be free from it. The body is then experienced as a prison. Spiritual dualism forges this estrangement into an ideology that denigrates the physical realm as the "lower" element in a hierarchical system. But if we abandon the body, we sacrifice our feelings, and with them our capacity for self-expression and relatedness to others.

Our being made from dust also means that we are social beings from the very beginning. Our interrelatedness is a fundamental human factor. Anyone whose anthropology begins with the individual is not in harmony with the biblical tradition. We are made, created together. It is within our social existence that all the affirmations of the good creation are made, questioned, become true.

Any theology that eschews the body and the society in favor of some higher realm does not take seriously our being made from dust. Let me give some examples of what I mean. Billy Graham, in a television discussion of one of my favorite New Testament stories—the parable of the rich young man—managed to evade the issue of wealth and the questions about materialism posed by this story (Mark 10:17–22). Instead Graham turned this text into an account of a young man's decision for or against Jesus. Nowhere did Graham state that Jesus instructs the rich youth to "sell what you have, and give to the poor" (v. 21). Hearing Graham, no one could possibly surmise that this parable had anything to do with money.

I think that the parable of the rich young man is a story about psychic depression and where it comes from. The rich young man has what he needs, and much more besides, but he is disquieted by inner feelings of emptiness. The question he puts to Jesus points to his need for something beyond having and being fulfilled in a material sense. "What must I do to inherit eternal life?" he asks (v. 17). Or, to focus his question in contemporary terms, What shall I do with my life? How can I make my life more radical, less ambiguous, less fragmented, less of a compromise? What can I do to escape from the halfheartedness of my existence? Jesus' injunction to sell his possessions, to give to the poor, and to "come follow me" is a stringent test of the youth's sincerity in seeking spiritual satisfaction. We are told, however, that when faced with this prospect the rich young man's "countenance fell, and he went away sorrowful; for he had great possessions" (v. 22).

The rich youth *could* enter into the fullness of life. The question he asks Jesus indicates his awareness that something is lacking, that he can expect more from life. But something is radically wrong with his notion of eternal life in the first place. He thinks: I have everything; I have obeyed all the rules; only one thing is missing: spiritual fulfillment. If I can only have food for the soul as well, everything will be fine. But Jesus turns his expectation upside down: You don't have too little, you have too much. Your material overabundance is the barrier between you and God. Yet in Graham's version this text is concerned exclusively with the soul, the will, and the decision for or against Jesus. Graham never once mentioned the wealth of this youth or his depression. Graham's interpretation of this story demonstrates that the "dust factor" eludes him.

In the same vein, I recall a sermon preached by a well-dressed, elegant woman in a cathedral in New York City. Talking about creation, she spoke about her cruise to South America, crossing the equator, the open sky, and the marvelous beauty of the southern hemisphere. She was praising the splendor of creation, and the words she used to conclude her description were "It's all ours. It has all been given to us." I was shocked. Hers was not a bodiless, rarefied spirituality but a bodily, sensuous spirituality bereft of any understanding of the social reality in which we live. Hers was an upper-class sermon without any consciousness of class reality, neither that of others nor that of her own. She displayed no awareness of those who live in the countries into which she ventured. She gave no thought to the people in Chile, but spoke in elaborate language about Chile's impressive terrain from the perspective of a tourist. When she said, "It's all ours," I wanted to walk out.

She did not realize what she was saying, but what I heard her say was that it was all ours to exploit and dominate; "it's all ours," and whoever opposes us has to be silenced, tortured, and killed; "it's all ours," because the whole world has been created for the enjoyment of upper-class tourists.

A genuine affirmation of God's good creation encompasses more than a tourist's perspective. To love God's good earth is to know about the hunger and exploitation of those who share the earth with us. Idealistic spirituality is blind not only to bodily reality but even more so to social reality. Affirmations of beauty lack truth if they exclude the vast majority of our brothers and sisters. They are false praises, mere abstractions that are isolated from reality.

The claim of Christian theology is that we are created, willed, and loved by God; yet we are made from dust. How then can we affirm creation and our having been created without making an idealistic leap away from the dust, the earth, the body, and the society? This is the problem. We have to examine any theology in terms of the extent to which it takes seriously our being made from dust or, in other words, our biological, socioeconomic reality. A theology that ignores our being made from dust constitutes an idealistic flight from reality and becomes, sooner or later, an ideological superstructure separated from the fabric of our lives. A theology that neglects our being made from dust is meaningless for our real needs and hopes. It diverts us from our historical project of liberation. The effort to deny the earth in orthodox Christian theologies represents a helpless idealism combined with a practical materialism. Much of Christianity is in this state right now. Many churches cannot cope with all the problems they face. Those that are honest admit that they are helpless, that they do not know what to do or say. So many church people are depressed. Why? Is it so difficult to have hope or to engage in the historical project of liberation? Helpless idealism has become a sort of ideology coupled with practical materialism—greed and selfishness.

The second maxim that is useful for an embodied theology is "The earth does not belong to the human being, but the human being belongs to the earth," a quotation from Chief Seattle. Historically our relationship to nature has been shaped by a ruthless imperialism over nature. As lords over the earth, we have turned nature into a marketable commodity. As if we could produce more earth, we treat it as an object of financial speculation. The laws of capitalistic production are applied to the land. The capitalistic understanding of the relation between the producer and the objects he or she sells is transferred to our relationship to the earth. The relationship is characterized by our ability to dominate, to produce more, and to sell more.

After completing his studies, Karl Marx became a journalist in Cologne. As a reporter for *Rheinische Zeitung* in 1842, he discovered that an increasing number of people were being prosecuted for theft. The young Marx wondered what this rising incidence of theft was all about and why people had all of a sudden become so immoral. It turned out that the state had enacted a new law which forbade the poor from collecting firewood from the forests. Previously the poor had roamed freely through the forests in search of wood, especially dead wood, for their ovens. They considered the forests free spaces. They were operating under the assumption that the earth belonged to God and that therefore they could partake of it. Suddenly their customary activity amounted to thievery. This story from Marx's time offers an excellent example of how capitalism alters our relationship to the earth. In preindustrial times, part of the land was free, woods were free, the waters were free. It is necessary to think in preindustrial terms (and to search for a postindustrial solution) if we are to understand what it means to say that the earth does not belong to some individual owner but that we belong to the earth.

Our ecological imperialism has its roots in the mind/body split, which in turn has spawned other dichotomies: the human versus the animal, man versus woman, adult versus child, the master race versus the slave race, intellectual versus manual work. All these dichotomies are based on a distorted understanding of creation. These dichotomies reinforce belief in the superiority of mind over matter and legitimate domination over the subjected. We must find a way to express our relationship to creation and to the creator that differs from the hierarchical ordering of reality into higher and lower components.

The earth does not belong to us. It is not something that we are allowed to plunder and exhaust at will. On the contrary, it is the human being who belongs to the earth, and to belong means to live in mutual dependence. We are dependent on the earth, we cannot afford to live in opposition to the earth, we cannot disregard the earth. Yet we continually try to deny or to expunge our dependence on the earth. We live against the rhythms of day and night, summer and winter, sleep and wakefulness. In the industrialized West, we tend to resist the natural rhythms of the earth or to forsake them, but it is impossible to cease living in relation to all natural rhythms without damage to ourselves. We are not absolutely independent. We must affirm our dependency on our mother, the earth. Actually it is more accurate to speak of an interdependency between humanity and the earth, for we are the stewards of the earth.

The third maxim, "La tierra es al Señor," or "The earth is the Lord's," was first used as a call to struggle for liberation by peasants attempting to overthrow European feudal rulers during the Middle Ages. Contemporary Latin American peasant revolts use the same biblical phrase to express their concept of the earth as common ground and not the sole possession of a handful of individuals. The call for redistribution of the land has been a major source of conflict in contemporary Latin America. Those who use the land are attempting to take it away from those who merely have paid for it. Peasants have challenged ruling elites who claim that the earth belongs to those who have paid for it and who therefore think that the earth is a marketable commodity.

It is a sacrilege to make the earth into a commodity. The earth does not know "mine" or "thine." The concept of the earth as God's good creation and the concept of the earth as private property are mutually exclusive. If the earth belongs to anyone, it belongs to those who actually use it and not to those who simply own it. It is the workers who participate in God's creation, not the absentee landlords. The workers create all that we use. Nicaraguan priest Ernesto Cardenal asks us to note:

> The shoes we wear were made by workers. The clothes, by other workers. The cities and everything in them and the highways and the bridges. . . . The workers continue the power of God on earth by working on creation. That's why the workers should be the owners of the earth and not the ones who don't do any work—the ones who have shoes and food and clothing and travel everywhere and don't work or sow or produce anything. But they own the work of the others and the houses and the land.[9]

The earth belongs to those who work, not to those who pay. In this sense, the earth is God's and not the possession of anyone.

NOTES

1. Martin Buber, *I and Thou*, a new translation with a prologue and notes by Walter Kaufmann (New York: Charles Scribner's Sons, 1970), p. 69.

2. Charles Hartshorne, *The Divine Relativity: A Social Conception of God* (New Haven and London: Yale University Press, 1948), p. 20.

3. Isabel Carter Heyward, *The Redemption of God: A Theology of Mutual Relation* (Washington, D.C.: University Press of America, 1982), p. 6.

4. Ibid.

5. Ibid., p. 2.

6. Ibid., p. 7.

7. Ibid., p. 41.

8. Plato, *The Last Days of Socrates*, trans. Hugh Tredennick (Harmondsworth, Eng.: Penguin Books, 1969), p. 112.

9. Ernesto Cardenal, *The Gospel in Solentiname*, trans. Donald W. Walsh (Maryknoll, N.Y.: Orbis Books, 1976), pp. 5–6.

4

Created in God's image

Following a chapel service I led at Union Theological Seminary in New York City, a friend approached me, hugged me warmly, and said, "Dorothee, my co-creator!" These words blew my mind. No one had ever said this to me before. I had heard the word "co-creation," but I had shunted it aside as an abstraction; it was never concrete enough for me. And "co-creator" was certainly not a word I would have used in a personal sense. Never would I have referred to a friend or an acquaintance as my co-creator. That would have seemed excessive to me, even arrogant. The truth was that I had had only an intellectual grasp of the meaning of this word and not an existential sense of it. Hearing the name of co-creator bestowed on me heightened my awareness of my own creative power. Creative power is something we all have but often ignore or relinquish. My creative power is my power to renew the world for someone or for a community. Through it I attempt to rebuild the house of life out of the ruins in which we now live.

One premise underlying my concept of co-creation is that the first creation is unfinished. Creation continues; it is an ongoing process. We fail to apprehend the meaning of creation if we reduce it to something that happened once upon a time. The image of God as "the clockmaker"— a god who created a monumental, automatic, perpetually self-winding artificial clock and then disappeared into eternity—still persists in the minds of many people today. This is deism; it is not Christian faith. To take creation seriously requires something quite different from a naive belief in an ever-reliable "clockmaker." If we would genuinely embrace creation, we must confront nothingness.

The tradition teaches us that God created everything out of nothingness. No world existed before God commenced creating the universe; there was only chaos and nothingness. But to say that creation continues is, among other things, to understand that chaos and nothingness are still with us and threaten to destroy "the house of being." The presence of nothingness is a basic fact of human, not just divine, life. We experience two forms of nothingness. One is the void within ourselves, which we typically confront for the first time during our adolescent search for an identity. The discovery of an inner emptiness produces in us a mixture of dread and fascination. We recoil from the void within ourselves, but we are also irresistibly drawn to it, just as when we stare into an abyss from a mountaintop we are repelled, then lured, by the power of the nothingness, the vast empty space before us. Only by confronting the nothingness within ourselves can we aspire to a new act of creation. And only if we participate in creation can we overwhelm the death wish that creeps out of the nothingness.

The other form of nothingness we experience, which is interconnected with the first, is the destructiveness and evil that characterize our world in a transpersonal sense. Because there is the threat of nothingness, a killing, destructive power in the world, we must continue creation. To become involved in the work of co-creation means dealing with the nothingness that threatens to swallow us up. The task of co-creation is not tantamount to planting flowers in the garden and feeling good about it. Co-creation means a little more than that. Those involved in the work of co-creation have to face the nothingness that is in us and surrounds us. Each nuclear bomb is a threat to undo creation and a harbinger of nothingness.

Creation and nothingness are not the sole province of God. We, not just God, confront the specter of nothingness in any authentic creative act we undertake. And through our novel and healing acts we continue the unfinished creation. The tradition, however, teaches otherwise. A theological distinction is always drawn in traditional teaching between "creating" and "making." The act of making is attributed to human beings and involves producing objects out of given materials. The act of creating is reserved for God because God created the universe out of nothingness. Our perception of the divine-human relation has been distorted by the equation of the divine with creation and nothingness and the consignment of humanity to the rudimentary realm of making.

Underlying the theological distinction between creating and making is the fear that God, as a result of human development, will become less important, that human creativity detracts from the power of the divine presence. But we are mistaken if we assume that the life of the creator diminishes as "the created" live more fully. The power of life is not a flat sum that must be divided, unequally, between the creator and the created, although mainstream theology often conveys this strange impression. On the contrary, the more a person develops her creativity, delves into the project of liberation, and transcends her own limitations, the more God is God. God does not cling to creational power, making it his possession, but shares it knowing that good power is shared power.

Although the Hebrew Bible uses the verb "to create" only in relation to God, it contains bold descriptions of human action using metaphors for creational power, such as the ones we find in Isa. 58:6–12:

> Is not this the fast that I choose:
>   to loose the bonds of wickedness,
>   to undo the thongs of the yoke,
> to let the oppressed go free,
>   and to break every yoke?
> Is it not to share your bread with the hungry,
>   and bring the homeless poor into your house;
> when you see the naked, to cover him,
>   and not to hide yourself from your own flesh?
> Then shall your light break forth like the dawn,
>   and your healing shall spring up speedily;
> your righteousness shall go before you,
>   the glory of the Lord shall be your rear guard.
> Then you shall call, and the Lord will answer;
>   you shall cry, and he will say, Here I am.
>
> If you take away from the midst of you the yoke,
>   the pointing of the finger, and speaking wickedness,
> if you pour yourself out for the hungry
>   and satisfy the desire of the afflicted,
> then shall your light rise in the darkness
>   and your gloom be as the noonday.
> And the Lord will guide you continually,
>   and satisfy your desire with good things,
>   and make your bones strong;
> and you shall be like a watered garden,
>   like a spring of water,
>   whose waters fail not.

And your ancient ruins shall be rebuilt;
  you shall raise up the foundations of many generations;
you shall be called the repairer of the breach,
  the restorer of streets to dwell in.

In these verses Isaiah describes the work of justice in terms of creation: "to loose the bonds of wickedness, to undo the thongs of the yoke, to let the oppressed go free . . . then shall your light break forth like the dawn. . . . You shall be called the repairer of the breach, the restorer of streets to dwell in." Every time I venture into places like parts of Harlem, I recall Isaiah's vision of "the restorer of streets to dwell in." There are about fifteen million jobless people in the United States right now, and yet so much work needs to be done to reconstitute the world from the ruins of our existence. Who will be the "repairer of the breach" and "the restorer of streets to dwell in"? Who will continue creation?

Isaiah 58:6–12 shows that doing justice and "breaking every yoke" is the way we become co-creators. Then our light breaks forth like the dawn. It is the light of those who pour themselves out for the hungry that will rise in the darkness. Isaiah also uses the image of a watered garden, which is evocative of paradise and its four streams. "You shall be like a watered garden, like a spring of water, whose waters fail not," says the prophet. All this natural imagery—light, noonday, water—serves to underscore the concept of a creation that continues to lighten the darkness. We are called to participate in creation, which is not an accomplished fact of our past but constitutes our very future. As co-creators, we participate in the goodness of creation when we undo evil.

If creation continues by virtue of our participation in it, what does this mean for our understanding of God? Carter Heyward arrives at this conclusion:

> God is "no one" but is rather a transpersonal spirit, power in relation, which depends upon humanity for making good/making justice/making love/making God incarnate in the world. To do so is to undo evil. The doing of good and undoing of evil is a human act, a human responsibility. God is our power to do this.[1]

Power-in-relation works through us. Arguing that "any creative relation is *mutually-messianic*,"[2] Heyward shifts our expectations for a divine messiah who would be our God but not our friend, to a God-human relation characterized by the mutuality of friendship and empowerment.

Although the concept of God as power-in-relation sounds heretical from a traditional perspective, it has solid scriptural grounding. The biblical expression that approximates Heyward's understanding of creative relationality is holiness. The word "holy" applies to both God and humanity. In the context of the giving of the commandments, God says to Moses: "You shall be holy; for I the Lord your God am holy" (Lev. 19:2). This theme recurs in Matthew 5: "You are the light of the world (v. 14) and "You, therefore, must be perfect, as your heavenly Father is perfect" (v. 48). The traditional concept of holiness pertains to our co-creative role with God in alleviating human suffering and making justice in the world. But is there any need for people in Western culture "to be more holy," as a black American spiritual puts it? Is there anyone who wants to sing, "Lord, I want to be more holy in my heart?"

In 1983, I had a perplexing experience in the classroom of a liberal arts college. The class was exploring the meaning of human suffering, death, and dying. They had read my book on suffering. When I arrived I felt a certain tension in the room. "What are the boundaries of suffering?" was the first question I heard, from a shrill voice that belonged to an attractive, healthy-looking young woman of eighteen. Had she ever experienced genuine suffering in her life, I wondered. "How far should we go in response to suffering?" she queried. I chose not to respond directly to her questions in order to flush out the reaction of the class as a whole to my perspective on suffering. Some of the students felt that I demanded they take on all the sufferings of the world. The young woman who questioned me initially felt overwhelmed by my implicit request that she immerse herself in the sufferings of other people, particularly the sufferings of the Third World, sufferings that we in the First World, as I pointed out to her, largely create. Once more, now angrily, she pressed me: "Doesn't this have to stop somewhere? Where are the boundaries?"

At that moment, the New Testament story came to mind where Peter asks Jesus, "Lord, how often shall my brother sin against me, and I forgive him? As many as seven times?" Jesus replies, "I do not say to you seven times, but seventy times seven" (Matt. 18:21–22). I had no sooner finished telling this story when I was bombarded with indignant responses from several students. "I am not Jesus." "Forget about Jesus." "What do you expect us to be? Do you expect us to be saints?" The debate was superficial, because we never explored the real causes of suffering. What this debate conveyed to me were the well-developed defense mechanisms of these young people in relation to the suffering of others, their rejection of any responsibility whatsoever for suffering, and the absence of any feeling of solidarity with other people and other cultures. My wish, to be holy because God is holy, stood alongside the vehement refusal of these students to confront suffering, especially the suffering of others. When someone called out, "I am not Jesus," I, feeling intimidated, nevertheless shot back, "Why not?" Why not try to live differently? Why not try to be co-creators and co-sufferers at one and the same time? This class displayed a glaring, practical lack of anything we might call faith, trust, holiness, transcendence.

A quintessential moment in the history of religion is the time God says in Lev. 19:2, "You shall be holy; for I the Lord your God am holy." The directive is clear: We, not only God, are destined to be holy. We are beckoned to approximate God. We are invited to acquire and practice the quality of holiness that characterizes God by doing the work of love and justice. Knowing Yahweh means doing justice. Based on this understanding, the Jewish tradition emphasizes the imitation of God. The Talmud explicitly states that we are able to imitate God's actions: "It is possible to imagine that man can be as holy as God."[3] The Jewish tradition, however, also ascribes to God a holiness which surpasses that of the human being: "My holiness is higher than any degree of holiness you can reach." But the rabbinical insistence on the supreme holiness of God still does not negate the emphasis on our human capacity for holiness. Created in the image of God, we therefore are able to imitate God. "What means the text, 'Ye shall walk after the Lord your God?'" In answer to this rhetorical question, the Talmud replies that the meaning of the text is "to follow the attributes of the Holy One, blessed be He: as He clothed the naked, so do you clothe the naked, as He visited the sick, so do you visit the sick. . . ."[4] Again and again the Talmud quotes different parts of the Hebrew Bible to underscore the idea that it *is* possible to imitate God. Remembering our Jewish religious roots is one way of restoring our trust in human beings, who are created, as the psalmist says, "a little less than God" (Ps. 8:5).

In the Bible there are many positive images and affirmations about the human being which speak to us about the holiness of life, the wholeness of human life, and about God-with-us and our being one with God. We are not mere vessels into which something like grace is poured; on the contrary, we are living parts of active love. A stirring commentary on the Lord's Prayer by a Nicaraguan peasant woman is recorded in Ernesto Cardenal's *The Gospel in Solentiname*. To the petition "Holy be your name" she responded:

> To make something holy then doesn't mean to chant, to say prayers, to have processions, to read the Bible. Making the name of God holy means to love others, to do something for others. If we set to glorifying God just with prayers and processions as we used to, we're not making God holy at all. In other words, to make love real is to make the name of God holy or to make his person known here on earth, even though maybe the name of God won't even be mentioned.[5]

The woman's understanding of God's holiness stresses not separation but unification between God and the human being. To make something holy is to make justice real. Cardenal suggests that "Holy be your name" might be better translated as "May your person be made known" or "May you be acknowledged (doing justice)."[6]

Many Protestant denominations deny human beings the power to imitate God in doing justice. Instead of celebrating our participation in creation, Protestantism emphasizes the unchangeability of the world and human sinfulness. Many Protestant theologies have concluded that we cannot change because we are so evil and because we have no power. This deprecatory talk cuts us down and severs us from faith and participation in God's good creation. The deeply ingrained anthropological pessimism of most Protestant denominations has no basis in the Jewish affirmation of our being created as images of God, empowered to grow into love and to become love ourselves. One of the tasks for theology in our time is to overcome this anthropological pessimism which denies our co-creatorship with God.

In the history of Christianity there are two opposite theological concepts of the God-human relation that may be differentiated under the rubrics of "otherness" and "sameness." Under the former rubric, God is the "wholly other"; under the latter, God and humanity may achieve a mystical union. If God is the wholly other or the stranger, as Hegel called God in his early writings, then God, as Hegel put it, is a stranger who rules over estranged people.[7] God's otherness makes God into a stranger and estranges humanity on earth. People do not feel at home; instead they wander like Abraham. It is clear that under the "otherness" rubric the distance between God and humankind is indefinite and unbridgeable. John Calvin and Karl Barth, for example, both display an overweening fear of sameness, of the possibility that someone might come too close to God or, worse yet, achieve a mystical union with God. Orthodox Protestantism deeply fears the possibility of sameness, of the identification of God with humanity, and therefore it fears mysticism. Mysticism is seen as an idolatrous deification of the human being. In orthodox Protestantism, God is understood primarily as a person, more specifically as a father, who above all demands obedience. This is the ethical implication of God's wholly otherness. If God is the other, then the basic thing he wants from us is obedience. Our salvation is then dependent on our obedience to the will of God. Under this rubric, salvation is construed as forensic justification. God or Christ declares the sinner justified, that is, saved. Salvation hinges on a freely willed act of God, who in the name of a judge passes final sentence on the crestfallen sinner. Sin here amounts to idolatry and disobedience.

Under the "sameness" rubric, the emphasis is on the God with us, the God within us, and the God with whom we can identify and finally be united. The images invoked by this tradition are often taken from nature—God as the depth, the abyss, the source of life, the water, the ocean. In mystical terms, salvation is equivalent to union with God, and therefore, in contrast with the "otherness" rubric, sin is alienation and

Otherness	*Sameness*
Infinite distance	Mystical union
God as the wholly other, stranger	God within us, the birth of God in the soul
Father image	Depth, abyss, ocean, source
Obedience to God	Empowerment by God
Salvation: forensic justification	Salvation: sanctification and union with God
Sin: idolatry, disobedience	Sin: alienation, emptiness
Orthodox Protestantism	Mysticism

emptiness. Sin is much more a matter of despair than of disobedience and idolatry. Sanctification, not mere justification, is the result of salvation. That we are created in the image of God connotes neither the total mystical union between God and humanity nor the total otherness of God. However, any good theology contains a mystical element. It is almost impossible for any theology totally to deny God's empowerment of us.

When we understand God as power-in-relation and ourselves as being empowered, then we are inspired to testify to the goodness of creation. There is a growing need among Christian feminists and others involved in liberation struggles to develop new ways of celebrating our own createdness and that of the world. Old terminology, in the mode of "Praise the Lord, the Almighty," will no longer suffice. We are in search of a different language, because the traditional language of praise does not work for us, and the contemporary inability to praise creation, the silence that comes out of despair, is not acceptable either. Both old religious and secular language do not satisfy the need I sense in many groups to develop a spirituality of creation. We are still in search of a new God-language and a way to express our ultimate concerns. Power-in-relation is a name Carter Heyward has given to God. I would like to encourage the reader to find her own names for God, to share them with others, and so participate in the human religious venture of naming who God is for us.

One of my favorite Bible stories is the healing of the epileptic boy in Mark 9. It is a story of the helplessness and powerlessness experienced by Jesus' disciples, who when approached by the father of the sick boy are unable to cast the demon out. They stand paralyzed before the suffering of the possessed son and his grieving father and consequently are subjected to the scorn and ridicule of a group of scribes and Pharisees in public. When Jesus comes on the scene, instead of consoling his friends, he makes clear to them that their inability to heal the boy signifies their lack of faith. He pronounces them a "faithless generation." If they believed in the power of life, they would participate in that power and thus be able to do what they think only Jesus can do: perform a miracle. And when the boy's father fervently beseeches Jesus to heal his son but qualifies his appeal with "if you can do anything," Jesus rebukes him as well: "If you can! All things are possible to him who believes" (Mark 9:23). In other words, when will you finally abandon this if-you-can talk? When will you finally give up your impotence, your weakness, your unbelief in the healing power of God? When will you begin to do God's work, feeding the hungry, healing the sick, and casting out demons? When will you discover that all is possible to her who participates in God's power? I learned from this story that one of God's names is "All-is-possible," and I know that if I cannot talk to All-is-possible, if I do not listen to All-is-possible, if I do not believe in All-is-possible, then I am dead. Thus my prayer would be to ask All-is-possible to be present.

In my own search for a new language of celebration, I am struck by the fact that verbs, not nouns, spring to mind. I need to wonder, to be amazed, to be in awe, to renew myself in the rhythm of creation, to perceive its beauty, to rejoice in creation, and to praise the source of life. Listing these verbs reminds me of people who believe that God has created them and all creatures, who trust in the goodness of creation. I cannot forget, however, all my brothers and sisters who have never learned to wonder, to be amazed, to renew themselves, and to rejoice. I think of those whose experiences do not lead to a deep trust and a belief in the goodness of creation. In German there is a colloquial expression for the people I have in mind—he or she is a *kaputter Typ*. He or she is broken, tuned out, kaput, without meaning or function. The German word *kaputt* refers to a machine or a thing, not to an organic whole. In the world of the *kaputter Typ*, there is no sense of relatedness to other people. Relationships are disturbed or even nonexistent. The language of the broken one cannot reach another person. She is unable to express her feelings, and her perception of the world is absurdly reduced. Her action does not make use of her capacities. The broken person has no trust in creation, no sense of her createdness or the possibility of empowerment. The broken person has been socialized in a culture that threatens all the capacities of human beings to take in creation in wonder and in awe, in self-renewal and in appreciation of beauty, in joy and in expressions of gratefulness and praise. Who then is the *kaputter Typ*? I will not answer this question, because we know him too well. You know him as I know her. After a long talk with a depressed student, I, exhausted from listening to him, finally asked, "Was there anything in the last year about which you felt some joy?" His response was that even the word "joy" had not come to his lips for two years, and he added that, objectively speaking, he had no use for such a word. He had never learned how to wonder or to be amazed.

Philosophy began with wondering, *thaumazein*. Wondering is part of our day-to-day experience as well. I recall when my youngest daughter learned to tell time. One day, in utter joy, she exclaimed, "Look, Mom, this is a truly wonderful five before half-past-six!" Perhaps children are the greatest conveyors of amazement. They do not bypass anything as too trivial or mundane. They free us from our banal and dull perspectives. To affirm creation means to enter into the freedom of amazement and delight. Nothing is simply available, usable, or to be taken for granted. The broken person will counter, "What is so special about it? It has always been that way." His capacity to trivialize everything has surpassed his capacity to wonder. He is crippled by a "dryness of the heart," as the mystics termed it. He no longer wonders about the wonders of the world. Children and artists are teachers of a spirituality of creation. They recombine created things into a new synthesis, and they change triviality into wonder, givenness into createdness. Through them we unlearn triviality and learn amazement; we again see the magnolia tree, and we see it as if for the first time.

Another element essential to a spirituality of creation is the human capacity to perceive beauty. We are able to notice, to observe, to perceive in a purposeless way that we call aesthetics. In German, the verb "to perceive" is *wahrnehmen*. Its literal meaning, which is "to take something as true," demonstrates that perception is related to truth. Our aesthetic perception lures us into truth. When "the doors to perception are cleansed," as Blake put it, we see more and we perceive the created world in a different way. The world appears no longer as disposable dead stuff but as a vital growing organism. In aesthetics we are all animists who believe that there is a soul in every living being. Our perception of aesthetic objects makes them responsive. A dialogue ensues between the perceiver and the otherwise inanimate object. We grasp the interrelatedness of creation in this dialogue between the sun and me, the birch and me. Perhaps then we see as God saw in the beginning when she said, "It is very good." The Hebrew word for good, *tov*, also means fair or beautiful. Thus God said on creating the universe, "Behold, it is all very beautiful." To love creation means to perceive its beauty in the most unexpected places. An aesthetic education that deep-

ens our perception is not a luxury for the elite but a cultural necessity
for everyone. To believe in creation is to perceive and to engage in the
aesthetic mode of perception. One cannot love God if one does not
know what beauty is:

> Ernesto Cardenal,
> questioned on how he came to be
> a poet, a priest,
> and a revolutionary,
> gave as his first reason
> love of beauty.
>
> This led him, he said,
> to poetry
> (and beyond);
> it led him
> to god
> (and beyond);
> it led him
> to the gospel
> (and beyond);
> it led him
> to socialism
> (and beyond).
>
> How weak a love of beauty must be
> that is content with house beautiful;
> how trivial a love of poetry
> that stops with the text;
> how small a love of god
> that becomes sated in him
> not hungrier;
> how little we love the gospel
> if we keep it to ourselves;
> how powerless are socialistic yearnings
> if they fear
> to go beyond what will be.[8]

The most terrifying quality about the life of the broken person—
both the one I meet and the one I am—is the absence of joy. In the
Jewish tradition, joy was understood as the most natural response to
our having been created, while sadness was deemed a rejection of the
gift of life. In this metaphysical sense, joy is not derived from special

events or the presents we receive; it involves the mere delight in being alive and gratefulness for the gift of life. But for an increasing number of people in secular culture the expression "a gift of life" does not make too much sense: If the giver disappears, why should we see life as a gift at all, why should we not understand it instead as a biological accident, a casual event, an unforeseen occurrence that neither has nor requires an explanation? When life has lost its quality of being something given to us, it turns into a mere matter of fact. People grow up in this culture without any education for joy. Does the deep, reasonless joy of being alive die in a world without religion? Does it make a difference with regard to our capacity for enjoyment whether we live in a world we think is made by human beings or in one we believe to be created by God? I do not know the answer to these questions, yet I observe a remarkable absence of joy in secular, industrialized cultures. At the same time, my own spiritual experience teaches me that to recall creation, to be reminded of our createdness in a community of people who struggle together, enhances my own awareness of joy—of how much I need it, how much I yearn for it. A spirituality of creation reminds us that we were born for joy.

These elements of a creation-centered spirituality—wonder, renewal, a sense of beauty, and the capacity to rejoice—are integrated into the act of praising creation. To love someone is, among other things, to praise the person we love. To laud is another purposeless action of which only the human being is capable, at least consciously. The early church fathers said that even animals laud God, but without awareness. If we are in love with someone, we are seized by the need to make our love explicit, to speak about the beloved one. We rush to discover a language in which we can praise the beloved. Could it be that we are in love with creation, as God is according to James Weldon Johnson's poem? If this is true, then it is not enough to think about nature's beauty; we have to articulate it. Our feelings become stronger and clearer when we express them. We become better lovers of the earth when we tell the earth how beautiful it is. It takes time to learn how to praise the beauty of creation. On the way, we rekindle our gratitude and shed the self who took creation for granted. We recover the sense of awe before life; we recover the lost reverence and passion for the living. This is not a saccharine, superficial form of spirituality.

I am reminded of an incident that occurred while I was teaching a class on mysticism which illustrates for me what a creational spirituality is and is not. A group of students had prepared a session on Francis of Assisi. They read aloud from his "Canticle of Brother Sun":

> Praised be You, my Lord, through Brother Wind,
> and through the air, cloudy and serene, and every kind of weather
> through which You give sustenance to Your creatures.
> Praised be You, my Lord, through Sister Water,
> which is very useful and humble and precious and chaste.
> Praised be You, my Lord, through Brother Fire,
> through whom You light the night
> and he is beautiful and playful and robust and strong.
> Praised be You, my Lord, through our Sister Mother Earth,
> who sustains and governs us,
> and who produces varied fruits with colored flowers and herbs.
> Praised be You, my Lord, through those who give pardon for Your love
> and bear infirmity and tribulation.
> Blessed are those who endure in peace
> for by You, Most High, they shall be crowned.
> Praised be You, my Lord, through our Sister Bodily Death,
> from whom no living man can escape.[9]

The students then proceeded to show several slides of sunsets and the sea, accompanied by a pious commentary on "The Canticle" in traditional theological language. Other members of the class grew impatient with their incessant, euphonious praise. Finally I interrupted the leaders and asked: "If you really love Sister Water, can you then talk in a timeless language as if nothing had happened to her? If you really love Brother Wind today, can you then forget pollution? Can you be silent about acid rain in North America? If you love someone who is going to be killed right before your eyes, would you be able to continue talking about the beauty of creation? If you learned anything from St. Francis, can you imagine how he would speak today? Did you not notice that the sentimental strain of Franciscan spirituality kills the spirit of Francis and is a sellout to the official church? If you really love Sister Water, can you forget that our rivers are dying?" Praising creation is not just a matter of elevating its beatific aspects. Francis of Assisi also included Sister Bodily Death in his praises.

In her novel *The Color Purple*, Alice Walker presents a conversation between two black women about God which is one of the best texts on religion in contemporary literature that I know of. The exchange between Celie and Shug has a dual thrust. On the one hand, it is a critique of traditional religion, its God-talk and its God-image; on the other hand, it is an attempt to affirm God in a new manner.

Celie has lived her life with a God-image that she now recognizes is dubious in the extreme. When Shug asks what Celie's God looks like, she sheepishly replies, "He big and old and tall and graybearded and white. He wear white robes and go barefooted." His eyes are "sort of bluish-gray. Cool. Big though. White lashes. . . ."[10] This God represents the power that white people have over blacks and that men have over women. With the awareness that the God she has been praying to all her life is a white man comes the shocking realization that she detests, and no longer needs, this God who "sit up there glorying in being deaf. . . ."[11] Just as "white people never listen to colored, period,"[12] so this God has never listened to the cries of the black woman Celie, whose father was lynched, whose mother was deranged, whose stepfather raped her repeatedly, whose life, prior to meeting Shug, was stunted by unrelenting toil and humiliation. And yet Celie struggles with God. Her need for God persists past her burgeoning rejection of an outworn white male deity: "But deep in my heart I care about God. What he going to think. And come to find out, he don't think. . . . But it ain't easy, trying to do without God."[13]

Shug has already laid to rest her once negative and empty concept of God: "When I found out I thought God was white, and a man, I lost interest."[14] This realization, however, signaled the beginning of her religious journey, not the end. Inspired to move beyond "the old white man," Shug now challenges Celie with a full-blown conception of God that departs radically from white, patriarchal definitions:

Here's the thing . . . the thing I believe. God is inside you and inside everybody else. You come into the world with God. But only them that search for it inside find it. And sometimes it just manifest itself even if you not looking, or don't know what you looking for. Trouble do it for most folks, I think. Sorrow, lord. Feeling like shit.[15]

Hers is a creational spirituality. The dialogue between this God and Shug, who refers to God as "It" because "God ain't a he or a she,"[16] flows out of her awareness that everything in creation is of God. "Listen," she says to Celie, "God love everything you love—and a mess of stuff you don't."[17] Shug's God-talk is grounded in her experience as a woman and in her love of life.

Shug's exceptional reflections on the relationship between God and humans climax in a passionate affirmation of the source of all life: "But more than anything else, God love admiration. . . . I think it pisses God off if you walk by the color purple in a field somewhere and don't notice it."[18] God is not synonymous with omnipotent control; rather, God's power lies in sharing life with others. The admiration God loves is our sense of connectedness with the whole of creation. We all have difficulties with praising the God of creation. We all often walk by the color purple in a field and don't notice it. But God does not give up trying to lure us into oneness with all creation.

NOTES

1. Isabel Carter Heyward, *The Redemption of God: A Theology of Mutual Relation* (Washington, D.C.: University Press of America, 1982), p. 159.

2. Ibid., p. 163.

3. A. Cohen, *Everyman's Talmud* (New York: Schocken Books, 1975), p. 23.

4. Ibid., p. 211.

5. Ernesto Cardenal, *The Gospel in Solentiname*, trans. Donald D. Walsh (Maryknoll, N.Y.: Orbis Books, 1976), p. 209.

6. Ibid.

7. See G. W. F. Hegel, *Early Theological Writings*, trans. T. M. Knox and R. Kroner (New York: Harper & Row, 1948).

8. Dorothee Sölle, "Ernesto Cardenal," in *Revolutionary Patience*, trans. Rita and Robert Kimber (Maryknoll, N.Y.: Orbis Books, 1974), pp. 64–65.

9. Francis of Assisi, "The Canticle of Brother Sun," in *Francis and Clare: The Complete Works*, trans. Regis J. Armstrong and Ignatius C. Brady (New York and Toronto: Paulist Press, 1982), p. 39.

10. Alice Walker, *The Color Purple* (New York and London: Harcourt Brace Jovanovich, 1982), p. 165.

11. Ibid., p. 164.

12. Ibid., p. 166.

13. Ibid., p. 164.
14. Ibid., p. 166.
15. Ibid.
16. Ibid., p. 167.
17. Ibid.
18. Ibid.

5

Work and alienation

The alienation of human beings from themselves is a historical fact and not an inherent characteristic of human nature. This is the way the Hegelian-Marxist tradition asks us to understand alienation. Far from being an eternally valid attribute of human nature, alienation occurs within the arena of the historical human project, and it is here that it will endure or be overcome.

History is the product of humankind, and alienation, in the words of George Novack, "expresses the fact that the creations of men's hands and minds turn against their creators and come to dominate their lives."[1] The woodcut *Treadmill* by Walter Habdank, pictured on the opposite page, is an imagistic expression of this Marxist insight. The figure yoked to the treadmill exemplifies the enslavement of people by that which their masters call work. It tells the story of what happens when the creations of people's hands and minds turn against their creators and come to dominate their lives. The picture was sent to me by a friend who works as an editor in a publishing house—a job most people would consider highly desirable. He very often feels like this man in the treadmill, shuttling from place to place at a ferocious, mechanical pace. Everyone feels this way sometimes. The treadmill is a poignant image of work as a curse, yet this is what work means for the majority of the population. According to the dictionary, a treadmill is "a mechanism consisting of a belt wound around two cylinders, kept in motion by a man (or a beast of burden) forced to tread it, and formerly used as an instrument of torture."[2] The treadmill is an older, precapitalist image, much older than the promises of high technology that atrophy before our very eyes. Despite high technology's promise to free people from the drudgery of monotonous work, the technology we have created continues to squelch human life. Now the instrument—the machine—is the master, not the human being. The treadmill is still with us.

The treadmill stands for any monotonous round of duties that we must accomplish, but it is an especially apt image for those who are confined to repetitive, routine, unsatisfying jobs, such as clerks, cashiers, secretaries, housewives, and many industrial workers. We can learn something by examining what is conspicuously absent from the treadmill image of human work. The most noticeably missing ingredient is the product. We do not see the result of this work; we see only the worker working. We behold the work process, but no product is visible, which means that even the joy of producing something is snatched away from the worker. This is the touchstone of alienated labor: The worker does not envision the work, does not plan the product he or she creates. The kind of seeing essential to good work, in which the worker envisions something prior to creating it, is obliterated. In alienated labor, the worker neither envisions nor plans the product she creates. Those who produce are alienated from the fruit of their labor.

Another dimension of work absent from this image is progress. No progress is made on the treadmill. The daily cycle never changes. From nine o'clock to five o'clock, or whatever the time slot, the treadmill runs its course. Even where there is a variety of tasks, the tasks are in a way all the same because neither vision nor responsibility is entrusted to or expected from the laborer.

The image of the treadmill also conjures up the picture of a worker who has no control of time. Being in control of one's time or discovering and following one's own timing is an important part of a person's experience of freedom. As a young adult, the Jewish mystical thinker and Nazi resister Simone Weil worked as a day laborer in the Renault car plant and other factories in Paris because she wanted to experience with her own body what it was like to work as workers did, to labor under the same conditions, to eat the same food, to live in a similarly shabby dwelling, to earn the same pay. She had been a teacher but gave up her teaching job to go into the factory. In the diary kept about this experience, she observed that when she arrived at the factory, another time took over which was no longer her time.[3] She noted that all the workers felt the same way. They all knew that time was taken away from them, that there was another time which was absolutely controlled by the machine or the conveyor belt and which destroyed their own sense of time. The desire to experience more intensive or less intensive periods of time is natural. Our existence as beings in time requires that we form and shape our time. It is like breathing in and breathing out. Yet we are deprived of this very natural aspect of our lives by most work.

Another thing lacking in the image of the treadmill is a neighbor, a fellow worker. There is only a solitary figure harnessed to the mill. The image reveals the absence of sharing among workers. People do work together, of course, but they cannot cooperate in vital ways under such conditions. Giving and taking are squashed by the treadmill. The person in the treadmill can learn nothing. He does not grow through work, does not change through work. The creature in the treadmill only gets exhausted.

The posture of the figure in the treadmill is bent; it is a painful, unnatural posture. There is no room for stretching; he cannot stand up. It appears as if he were doomed to this miniature gallows for the rest of his life. This is a powerful expression of what work is—being forced into something smaller than we are or might be. Most people have to live like that. They are forced to live beneath their own level of physical, emotional, rational, and spiritual endowments. As the treadmill figure attests, people are crippled, bent, reduced on the gallows of work.

The highly expressive hands of the treadmill figure offer another glimpse into the nature of alienated labor. Human hands are a potent symbol of what work is. It is through his hands that the worker creates something new, something good. Yet the hands of the man in the treadmill are clawlike, gnarled, dangling from the wrists in despair, because these hands do not form, feel, or produce anything meaningful. There is no mind in these hands. The beauty of human hands is that there is intelligence in them. To use one's hands well requires the operation of the mind. Then mind and hand become one; they work together. But in the hands of the treadmill figure there is merely despair, just as there is in his face.

The worker is alienated from her product, which belongs to another person; from her productivity, which is dominated by others; and from her fellow human beings, because work in capitalist society pits people against one another. The majority of people are alienated from their productivity because it is dominated by others. The privilege I have over many other human beings is that I enjoy my work, I do what I want to do, I plan my work. There are times when I choose to refuse mindless tasks. At other times I am forced to do them. I am not absolutely free, but I do have a much greater degree of freedom than most people I know because of my professional status. A class system that accords privilege to the few and denies it to the many also breeds division and dissension among members of the same class. Solidarity and cooperation are effectively thwarted. Workers are through their work alienated from the human family as a whole.

I remember the time when those of us in the antiwar movement tried to convince our labor unions in West Germany to join the protest against the Vietnam War. Some Australian labor unions had already gone on strike over the war. This was one of the few strikes that has ever been carried out for political reasons. Because of the Vietnam War, the Australian dockworkers refused to load and unload American ships. We in the antiwar movement appealed to some union people to organize West German workers for a similar strike, but to no avail. Much more than at any other time before or since, I sensed the alienation from the human family that work in a capitalist society fosters. The union leaders we spoke with had no concern about the fate of yellow babies in Vietnam. The suffering of a people several thousand miles away did not touch them; they did not even think about it. By contrast, the old labor movement was an international movement from its beginnings, for whom solidarity implied something more than cooperation among fellow workers at the same factory on the same shift. Solidarity of course begins there, but its final destination is international in scope.

When the old labor movement sang the "Internationale," they expressed solidarity with the workers of the world, not just with the workers at a particular plant. They sang, "Arise ye prisoners of starvation, arise ye wretched of the earth / for justice thunders condemnation, a better world in birth." The "Internationale" pays tribute to the understanding of humanity as one family and to the oneness of the human race. Central to the workers' movement of Marx's time was the understanding that the human species is something we share in common and that to be a human being is to be related to other people and especially to those who suffer from intolerable working conditions. Workers' solidarity was not bound to the nation state. The nation state was a bourgeois invention, whereas the solidarity of workers transcended such boundaries.

Mother Jones, one of the most remarkable women in U.S. working-class history, stood by the internationality of workers' solidarity. Born in 1830, she spent fifty of her one hundred years fighting fiercely on behalf of "her children," as she called the coal miners and other workers. In her autobiography, a series of anecdotes tape-recorded when she was over ninety years old, she tells the following story. She was speaking at a steelworkers' strike meeting in 1919 when a bystander began passing out leaflets about the blockade against Russia and the hunger, starvation, and disease that had resulted. The organizers of the strike tried to hinder this man when Mother Jones intervened. "What is the matter with these leaflets?" she asked. An organizer responded:

> Nothing, Mother, only if we allow them to be distributed the story will go out that the strike is engineered from Moscow. We can't mix issues. I'm afraid to let these dodgers circulate.[4]

In her wonderfully concise and clear manner, Mother Jones addressed the meeting:

> Women and children blockaded and starving! Men, women, and children dying for lack of hospital necessities! This strike will not be won by turning a deaf ear to suffering wherever it occurs.[5]

One cannot compartmentalize hunger, responding to the hunger of some but not to that of others. One cannot love children by choosing to love some while denying others. It simply does not work, as Mother Jones insisted.

The depoliticization of workers and their separation from other workers and the human family are forms of alienation that occur through work. There is a longstanding debate about the extent to which alienation is the novel result of industrialism or capitalism's wage labor system and at what point in history alienation set in. In *Phenomenology of the Spirit* Hegel explained why work, governed as it is by the master-slave relationship, automatically gives rise to human alienation.

The master appropriates and possesses the servant's labor. The servant is alienated from his own productivity because it is usurped by the master, whose supremacy rests solely on his owning the means of reproducing life, not on his own merits or accomplishments. To the master, the servant or wage laborer appears as just another object to be exploited.

Insofar as the wage laborer is owned by the master, she loses her identity. But by the same token, according to Hegel, the dialectical reverse occurs: The master, by living off the labor of the servant, relinquishes the means of his own self-realization through lack of productive activity. By contrast, the laborer, who develops her capacities and loses herself in work, actually wins herself back and is therefore stronger than the master. However much she is exploited and alienated, the laborer continues to produce and to realize herself through work. In making this significant discovery, Hegel pointed the way to a radical revision of the meaning and nature of labor. Marx later challenged Hegel's analysis by questioning the real empirical strength of the servant. Is the wage laborer genuinely stronger than his master, the owner of the means of production? Would the worker be able to achieve self-realization while suffering under the yoke of alienated labor? Whereas Hegel had analyzed the master-servant relationship in an agrarian setting, Marx's analysis arose from his observation of the imprisonment of the worker within an early industrialized, capitalist system that jeopardized the self-realization of the laborer.

If we are serious about acting as co-creators with God to fashion a more just world, then we must eliminate the evil of alienated labor. If we are serious about reflecting on work in a theological way, then we have to treat work as part of our being created in the image of God. And if we are earnest about this endeavor, then we have to de-ideologize ourselves from one of the most prevailing ideologies of our time, which is that work means paid work. Our ideological imprisonment vis-à-vis work is reflected in our identification of work with wage labor. Instead of viewing work as meaningful in itself, we relate work to compensation and value work according to its financial rewards. As we cleave to this ideology, we impoverish the meaning of work. We reduce it to a commodity, something devoid of meaning apart from the marketplace.

The purpose of work is to provide ourselves with the goods essential for our subsistence. But capitalism has completely transformed the worker's relation to work and productivity. In Marxist terms, capitalism has eliminated the use value of the product in favor of its exchange value, so that little by little everything we touch becomes exchangeable. A product is seen not in relation to the need it fulfills but in relation to the profit it can make. That which is not to be sold and paid for does not really exist in the ontology of profit and exchange value.

The primacy of exchange value is easily illustrated. For example, I am walking along the beach and find the most exquisite shell I have ever seen. I am happy with it. This is what Marx would call (in his instrumentalist language) its use value. Then I meet some people and show them what I've found. How do they react? "How lovely! It could be sold in a boutique!" one says. "How nice!" says another. "You should paint it and sell it." Or, "Wonderful! Now what will you do with it?" They respond as people who have internalized the meaning of exchange value. Their reaction is not to appreciate the joy, the pleasure I have in the shell but to transform it into something else to make a profit.

In a "natural" precapitalist society, different needs were met through different products that had a use value for the community. Labor is the mediation between need and product. Because our needs are different, unequal, and incomparable, labor is aimed particularly at the useful product. All three factors—needs, forms of labor, and products—are qualitatively different. My labor for my potatoes is different from your labor for your shoes. What happens in capitalism is that this qualitative difference disappears, first in regard to the product, which becomes a commodity with a specific exchange value, and second in relation to the corresponding form of labor, which loses its distinctive quality and becomes a mere abstraction. In other words, labor becomes quantified according to wage units. Even though the needs of people are by nature unexchangeable, both commodity and work have become quantifiable and abstracted from the needs of the human being. In this process, characteristic of capitalist society, we lose sight of both the use value of a product to satisfy a particular human need and the labor involved in producing the product as well. Marx invoked the term "abstraction" for our denial of the particularity of different forms of labor and the use value of their products.

This process of abstraction breeds amnesia about the aim of human labor. The self-expression of the worker by way of defining his or her needs, designing the work, and producing the product becomes impossible. All human needs are transformed into the one universal need for money. The exchange value of a product acquires an existence separate from its use value in the form of money. Hence, the old cycle of an earlier, "natural" economy, namely, commodity-money-commodity, is reversed to form a new cycle of money-commodity-money. The purpose of production, then, is no longer to satisfy human needs but to generate exchange value, specifically money, that meets our needs only in a mediated way. Under capitalism, exchange value creates exchange value, intensifying and escalating our alienation from the use value of what we produce.

An enormous amount of repression is required to adjust people to this process of abstraction and alienation; they have to quantify their qualitatively different needs and then forget or suppress them. The psychic costs of this process of repression and abstraction are immense. I will return to these costs in the chapter on sexual alienation. Here I will focus on how the process of repression destroys any sense of good work in terms of self-expression, relatedness to our neighbors, and reconciliation with nature.

The worker is alienated from the use value of his product when he does not know what he produces. The electronics industry provides an example. Its products are often military-related, yet there are workers, mothers of children, who work for this industry unaware that they are producing weapons of death. Unbeknown to them, their products serve the war machine. They have been alienated not only from the product of their work but from its purpose as well. These workers do not know that they are part of the military machine and that by producing these tiny electronic devices they have a hand in killing. Their understanding of their work is shaped almost exclusively by its exchange value. They have learned to evaluate their work according to their salaries. Good work pays more; inferior work pays less. No matter that the job is meaningless, injurious to others, inimical to one's self—its exchange value is the primary consideration before which all else pales. This kind of work robs workers of their dignity, turns them into machines, and destroys the collective sense of the person both as a creative being and as a responsible being. Thus unmoored from a sense of wholeness and purpose, people resign themselves to selling their work-power, their manpower, in the marketplace. They offer themselves for sale and scramble to salvage whatever shards of their identity remain. The worker must subject herself to the formal equality within commodity trafficking. She must adjust herself to the logic of exchange and profit, suppress her human feelings, and make calculating reason her own. This causes severe problems especially for women, who have been socialized to an entirely different set of values. In the world of exchange and profit, individuals are atomized and isolated from one another. Since their needs are suppressed and muted, relationships between workers in an exchange labor situation degenerate into exchange relationships. Social intercourse with each other can happen only when workers suspend their personal feelings in the process. All wishes, drives, and feelings are cut off in the exchange and trafficking of commodities. From the viewpoint of the rationally calculating manager, human needs appear as disruptive factors, as potential sources of error in the process of production. But this rational calculator, this foreman, does not operate only outside ourselves, controlling our work through time cards and the threat of being laid off or fired; his agents are also lodged in the psyche of each of us. We have internalized the rules of commodity production that demand rational calculation and the discounting of human feelings, both our own and others', as disruptive, useless emotions.

This kind of work is like prostitution. A prostitute relies on her customers' money. She may not display her feelings about her customers without imperiling her livelihood. If she dislikes her customer, if she finds him foolish, arrogant, foul-smelling, she is forced to endure him for money's sake. The same thing is true for the worker who is forced to market herself. Wage labor is a form of prostitution. Wage slavery is something that the old socialists understood. Their objective was not simply to increase the earning power of laborers but to transform the nature of work into something meaningful, in which workers would see the use value of their products, would employ the full range of their capacities, and would transmit and receive knowledge in the workplace. The wage labor system, as we know it, pays people to remain silent and to conform to the rules of the game.

That workers are paid for their conformity, however, does not sufficiently explain why whole populations in Western societies have allowed themselves to be so enslaved and have acquiesced to the loss of their human potential and their dignity in the labor market. How could whole populations so long endure the destruction leveled against them by the wage labor system? How can a system function that affronts the dignity of the majority of its members? Part of the answer to these questions lies in the fact that Western capitalism, to its credit, has increased the span of human life, ended mass subjugation to backbreaking forms of labor through the introduction of modern conveniences, and spawned a diverse flow of commodities and services that have freed up our collective human potential. Yet the majority of people are held hostage by a socioeconomic system that grants independence of thought and action to only the elite few. Those locked into subordinate positions by virtue of birth and education go against the dictates of the system at peril to their livelihoods. The vast majority of workers learn to suppress their personalities and aspirations because they simply cannot afford to forfeit the next paycheck. But it is not just money that ties a person to his or her place in the hierarchy. Most workers have been informed, successfully, that they are inferior to their educated, affluent managers. Somewhere below the level of consciousness they believe that the system that denies them greater participation in decision-making, greater control of their time and movements, a larger share of the profits, and self-expression is correct.

It is necessary to brainwash people before they will surrender their human dignity. Undergirding the reality of wage slavery is an ideological support system that encourages people to cooperate in their own dehumanization. Religion is one of the primary ideological tools used for this purpose. Religion ideologically abets and sustains the wage labor system through the Protestant work ethic, which arose together with capitalism.

The inspiration for the Protestant work ethic was the Reformation belief that our laboring is the will of God. The Protestant work ethic eschewed contemplation and upset the balance between contemplation and work by stressing the dignity of work. Work was reinterpreted in the Reformation as service to God, and the industrious worker was deemed the true servant of God. Work became a calling and at the same time the basis of self-worth. People received a new identity founded on their work. Being an industrious worker, working hard regardless of the quality of the work or the purpose it served, became a virtue in itself. Reformation religion recast harsh realities so that they could be tolerated. The interpretive, or "naming," function of religion, by which the most meaningless and routine work was pronounced a "calling" and the most exploitative work situation dubbed the place "God has given you," has since been discredited. Nevertheless, it has left an idelible imprint on us, and this is nowhere more evident than in the modern secular world's evaluation of employment and unemployment.

Workers in highly industrialized societies blame themselves, at least unconsciously, for having "lost" their jobs. Their self-worth is so inextricably bound up with employment that they readily conclude that the inability to keep a job is their own fault. Social scientists throughout the United States are discovering that today's unemployed, like their counterparts in the Depression of the 1930s, blame themselves for their joblessness. They account for rising rates of suicide, alcoholism, first-time admission to mental hospitals, homicide, wife-battering, and child abuse.[6] The jobless personalize greater economic forces and suffer from unemployment not only economically but psychologically.

The emergence of the Protestant work ethic did contribute to a new understanding of work that contained such constructive components as concern for the common good and insistence on the individual's right to make use of communal resources, but the concept of work that it spawned (which until recently went unexamined) is that work is good regardless of its substance. The overwhelming acceptance of this empty concept has cut us down. In a system in which any work is counted good no matter what it produces, the vast majority of work will mean alienation of the worker from the means of production, the mode of organization, the division of labor, in short, anything related to the use of the worker's productive powers. Equally as insidious as the concept of the goodness of all work is the fear that originally inspired it, the fear of sin. In the minds of the Reformers, human work was the antidote to idleness, which was considered the breeding ground of sin. Because work helped people resist temptations and worldly pleasures, it was essential for salvation.

If our obedience, to be demonstrated through work, is God's preeminent demand, then disobedience against the father, the owner, the boss, and behind these authority figures, God himself, is sin. The practical consequences of the otherness-of-God tradition discussed earlier (see

chapter 4) are evident in the social ethics of labor. Disobedience, re-
bellion, and critical protest are excoriated as the chronic symptoms of
idleness and therefore of sin, while mere functioning, emptiness,
mindlessness, and listlessness, which truly insult the creator of life, are
ignored. And by virtue of their socialization, women, more than men,
have been injured by a system that rewards passivity and punishes the
desire to experiment and innovate.

Although I do not consider the Protestant work ethic a curse, an ideology that keeps people down, I believe that today it functions in this
way. As a result the Protestant work ethic is crumbling. It just does not
function as well as it once did. Its values are no longer so easily internalized that they can be automatically handed down to the next generation. Many sons and daughters of industrious, disciplined workers are
reproaching their parents for their enslavement to work and their inability to find meaning and worth in any other aspect of life. It is a
healthy sign that today people are refusing to do some kinds of work
because they do not believe that just any work is good work. Their
refusal flies in the face of the Protestant work ethic, which was once
held intact by religion. It was once the pastor, and in the shadow of the
pastor, God, who suppressed the questions: Is this the work that I really want to do? Is this what I can do best? Religion has served to accommodate people to meaningless work.

Reinforcement of the wage labor system by the Protestant work ethic
as an ideology has had a disastrous impact on working people. It has reduced work to a duty, a meaningless duty, and demanded the unques-
tioning obedience of those who work. The worker has been educated
not to question, not to inquire into, the conditions of the workplace,
not to protest health hazards or the division of labor, and on an even
deeper level, not to question what work does to the worker.

NOTES

1. George Novack, "Introduction," in *The Marxist Theory of Alienation* by Er-
nest Mandel and George Novack, 3d ed. (New York: Pathfinder Press, 1976),
p. 7.

2. *New Webster's Dictionary of the English Language* (Chicago and New York:
Consolidated Book Publishers, 1975), s.v. "treadmill."

3. Simone Weil, "Factory Work," trans. Felix Giovanelli, *Politics* 3, no. 11 (December 1946): 369–75.

4. *The Autobiography of Mother Jones*, ed. Mary Field Parton, 3d ed. rev. (Chicago: Charles H. Kerr, 1976), p. 223.

5. Ibid., pp. 223–24.

6. See, e.g., Bryce Nelson, "Despair among Jobless Is on Rise, Studies Find," *New York Times*, April 2, 1983, p. A-25; and Donna Day-Lower, "Reworking the Work Ethic," *The Other Side* 19, no. 6 (June 1983): 10–13.

6

*Between paradise
and curse*

Although the nineteenth-century industrial revolution provoked some revisions of the Protestant work ethic, it never impelled people to break away from Protestantism's obeisance to labor. Once industrialization overturned the agrarian-based economy, labor was measured and rewarded monetarily, production became more competitive, and success became more quantifiable. The source of satisfaction, previously known to the agricultural worker, was no longer one's creativity in cultivating the land or in contributing to the life of the community. There emerged a secularized version of the Protestant work ethic in which the meaning of work was reduced to "making it."[1] In the preindustrial ethic, labor was defined in terms of ingenuity, participation in the common good, and even as opportunity for self-improvement apart from its financial rewards. By contrast, the secular, industrial ethic stripped labor of these values. Employment came to signify a class status and a moral status superior to that of the unemployed. Owing to this division, the remnants of the Protestant work ethic destroy what is most crucial in today's job crisis, namely, solidarity between the employed and the unemployed. The absence of solidarity is the identifying mark of alienated labor. Once solidarity is destroyed, work becomes a commodity that some people possess, others do not. The monolithic emphasis on financial compensation for work has undermined the other human values we once cherished in work, such as creative power and fulfillment, our relationships with other workers, and the transformation of and reconciliation with nature.

Marx believed that the alienation of the worker from his or her own work is the basis for all other forms of alienation. Marx therefore did not attribute our alienation to our general unhappiness in society, to the pendulum swings of our psyche, or to our childhood and what our parents did to us. Marx began with work and from there examined other factors figuring into alienation. It makes a difference whether we start with the collective fate of an entire class, a nation, a community, *or* with the individual. When we start with the individual, we have almost no recourse but to blame the victim—to tell the person that he or she could improve, could perform better, could suffer less, or could deal more effectively with her own instincts and feelings. But when we start with work as the source of alienation, or when our point of departure is our collective fate, then the solution to the problem of alienation will appear to be communal, concerted action to change the conditions of work.

Marx's economic analysis, rooted in his concept of alienation, is so valuable because it gives priority to labor over capital, unlike all liberal economic thought, which grants primacy to capital over labor. There are entire economic treatises devoid of even the most remote reference to the worker and what the worker does. The capitalist system is one in which capital breeds capital and the worker is subordinate to that end. But Marx viewed work as worthy of our deepest respect. For Marx, the person who genuinely delves into work is the human being in her or his most humane state. "Labor," "praxis," and "self-activity" are three interchangeable terms in the early writings of Marx. By labor in this positive sense, Marx meant self-directed activity and not other-directed activity, not wage slavery.

Most East European newspapers place tremendous emphasis on work. The front pages of the papers frequently contain news about the size of the year's potato harvest, the percentage of the harvest each collective was responsible for, and similar details that do not interest people brought up in a culture that devalues work and human labor and consequently does not discuss it very much. But again and again East European newspapers manifest a cultural respect for the human being as a worker, "the heroes of work" as they are called. This kind of respect is unheard of in Western culture, because we despise the worker just as much as, according to statistics, people despise or loathe their work.

The worker carries out the historical project of humanity. In theological terms, the worker is the living sign of ongoing creation. Alienation through labor is therefore an assault on creation itself; it denies the human project. To deny someone necessary and fulfilling work is to deny that person's being created in the image of God. To deny people work is synonymous with saying that they are exchangeable cogs in the machine, that they do not deserve their co-creatorship, which unfolds in labor, praxis, and self-activity, that is, activity which realizes the essential powers of the self. To make a commodity out of the self-affirmative praxis called work and our self-giving activity called love is to separate us from the source of life.

Sin is the state of alienation of the worker from his work, from his fellow humans, and from humanity's historical project. And the sinful deeds we primarily mean when we talk about sins in the plural follow from this basic alienation from God, from the source of life. From a Christian perspective, sin has two dimensions that are always in dialectical tension: fate and guilt. We are born into sin; it is a fate for which we are not personally responsible. But we are also guilty of committing sinful deeds. As victims of a situation that alienates us, we victimize others and alienate ourselves in return. Sin in a moralistic sense refers to evil deeds, personal fault, and guilt. Sin in an existential sense refers to lack of trust, emptiness, and the subjection of our lives to the vagaries of the status quo. Speaking of alienation as a modern term for sin is not an attempt to wash ourselves of guilt but to reconceive the interrelation between guilt and fate as they operate in human sin. To free ourselves from sin is a matter not just of doing better deeds but of changing the direction of our very beings in order to live new lives as co-creators with God. In a moralistic sense the sin of the human being as a worker is seen as laziness, lack of zeal and interest. But from an existential perspective sin is enforced labor, as a result of which the worker fails the human project of co-creatorship. Labor is unreconciled in our society. The destructiveness of bad work cannot be compensated by payment. The painful discrepancy between the reality of work and the human project of liberation cries out for reconciliation and forgiveness, which amounts to nothing less than systemic social change. If we understood what it meant to confess that we are sinners, our prayer would be for a social arrangement of good work that would reconcile us to the human project of creativity and freedom.

The alienation from our very being as workers furthers the predominant mood of powerlessness inside capitalist societies. "There's nothing we can do about it" is a customary response to, for example, the preparation for nuclear annihilation. It is the response of the nonbeliever. It is the response of the spiritually dead person. The measure of spiritual death is not whether people believe in God. Statistics indicate that a phenomenal proportion of American citizens believe in God, far many more than in Europe. But professed belief in God on a massive scale does not say anything when juxtaposed to the pervasive popular feeling of powerlessness that is the nonbeliever's perspective. "There's nothing we can do about it" is the voice of practical atheism. In the United States there exists a strange combination of theoretical theism and practical atheism. People believe in some supreme being "up there," but this heavenly being does not change anything here, neither in my heart, nor in my community, nor in the world. This combination of practical atheism and theoretical theism surfaces very visibly in work and in how people feel about their work.

We have to teach ourselves again to relate pleasure to work instead of connecting it with drudgery, dullness, and stupidity. In the creation narrative, the earthling Adam is put in the garden "to till it and keep it," according to Gen. 2:15. Phyllis Trible states that "since the garden of Eden is a place of delight, to till and to keep it is to foster pleasure."[2] Trible goes on to interpret "to till" as "to serve," with the connotation of respect, reverence, and worship. "To keep" the garden means to protect it. Both keeping and tilling, which are the first biblical references to human work and to the earth creature as a worker, "connote not plunder and rape but care and attention."[3] Work, as it is depicted in Genesis 2, is not a curse that descends on the human being after the Fall; it is, from the beginning, an expression of the human project of liberation, of its dignity and integrity. Through work, human life shifts from passivity to participation. This interpretation of work has so often been overlooked in the Christian tradition, which typically has held that work is *only* the result of sin. Orthodox Christianity has tended to disparage human work as a curse, as irrelevant to our salvation, as lowly in comparison with the magnificent works of the creative God. In the course of Christian history, God's magnificent work in creation has been used to humiliate, to belittle, human beings. Instead of giving dignity to the human being as a worker, the Christian tradition has often undermined the worker through talk of the fruitlessness and insufficiency of human work.

If we read the paradise story more carefully, we will see that work is an essential component of human life. Even the word "paradise," as a Persian borrowing originally meaning "fenced orchard," is a strong symbol of human work. In the center of the orchard the earthlings are created as workers to till and to keep the garden, and by doing so they keep themselves alive. Through work we not only give of ourselves, but simultaneously create and sustain ourselves. The biblical creation story reminds us of the goodness of work, apart from which there can be no belief in creation. As God worked six days and rested, so too the human creature is fulfilled in his or her co-creative responsibilities through work and rest. The most outstanding institution in Jewish religious life, the Sabbath, honors the alternation of work and rest. In keeping the Sabbath and celebrating its peace, the people of Israel affirm the goodness of work as an intrinsic part of creation. They counter the curse tradition of work as unending drudgery. In the Jewish tradition "labor is not only the destiny of man; it is endowed with divine dignity. . . . The Sabbath as a day of abstaining from work is not a depreciation but an affirmation of labor, a divine exaltation of its dignity."[4] It is not enough to love the sunset, to equate belief in creation with introverted, sentimental feelings about nature and its beauty. We also have to immerse ourselves in reality and understand the goodness of work and the dignity of the worker if we are to take our createdness seriously.

As noted earlier, the Christian tradition historically has focused on the concept of work as a curse that God inflicted on the earth, on the ground, and on the two original human beings. Hardship and difficulty accompanied work in the biblical account. According to the Bible, however, the disparity between human effort and success is not rooted in creation. The disparity was not originally intended by God, but rather emanated from human sin. Work as it is invoked by the "curse tradition" is separated from the goodness of tilling and keeping, from the dignity of co-creating, from the responsibility for the goodness of creation. In the "curse tradition," work is punishment. But is it true that the original disobedience of Adam and Eve destroyed all work as part of the goodness of creation so that we do not have any good work and are forced to view work in a purely negative light? Is this what Scripture tells us?

Interpreting the Genesis narrative as an etiological explanation for "original sin"—a term that does not appear in the story of the Fall—seems to be an all too orthodox reading of a myth that speaks about our development as responsible human beings who have to make choices between good and evil instead of living in a "dreaming consciousness," in the words of Kierkegaard. When a child learns to say no to her parents or other authorities, it is a sign of the humanness of this little person. She has chosen to be free by saying no. This is the only path by which she may be truly able, at a later point, to say yes. There is no yes without a no. Therefore the talk about the "disobedience" of Adam and Eve is misleading, as if they could have remained obedient just by refraining from eating the forbidden fruit of the tree of knowledge. We ought to cease understanding this confrontation with the authority of the father, this cutting of the umbilical cord, as sin. The story of the Fall is in many ways the story of a rise in human development rather than the story of our fall into guilt and sin. The myth mirrors the guilt all of us experience in growing up, making our own choices, leaving the commanding father who wants to keep his trees for himself along with the womb of our mother, symbolized by the nourishing waters of paradise and our symbiotic life within it. But there is no way to become an adult while remaining in a "dreaming consciousness" and in symbiotic attachment to the womb.

In the medieval German epic *Parzival* there is a moving scene in which the young boy Parzival leaves his mother Herzeloyde to become a knight. She has assiduously kept him away from courts and knights; she has warned him of the dangers of knighthood; she has secreted him in the woods; and, as a further safeguard, she has made him appear ludicrous by dressing him in a foolish-looking patchwork gown. But her efforts to keep him by her side are in vain. He leaves, and Herzeloyde dies of a broken heart. Parzival learns only later that his mother died when he departed.

This mythical story talks about what it means to grow up. There is no way to mature without breaking away from the parent, without causing pain to the one who remains behind, and without guilt. There is no painless or guilt-free path to adulthood, and this is what the biblical story of the Fall also tells us. The moral option we face is not a choice between obedience and disobedience. There is only one moral choice: to disobey, to eat of the tree of knowledge, and thereafter to live through the hardships of life.

It is a moral choice to contradict the authoritative voice of the parent God, to take the guilt on oneself in leaving a parent behind, and to embark on a new path. By affirming their right to choose, Adam and Eve become adults, at which point work and sexuality, though given with creation, take on a different and more complex meaning. Adam and Eve are now confronted with the consequences of being workers and lovers. And because they have changed through their courageous step, God the relational being also changes. God moves from parenthood to companionship. The biblical myth attests to a change in God's behavior. God does not condemn Adam and Eve to death (the punishment decreed in Gen. 2:17), nor does God completely abandon them. In spite of their failure to obey the commanding voice of the parental God, God supports them and makes clothing for them (Gen. 3:21). God surpasses God the demanding father. And it is this changed God who accompanies Adam and Eve as they exit from paradise. Having risked losing Eden's keeper, they come in touch with a new God.

While championing a form of obedience that idealizes a certain phase of childhood, Christian orthodoxy is possessed by a dread of disobedience. If we read the Bible in a more enlightened way—and here I draw on the excellent work by Erich Fromm *You Shall Be as Gods* for my insights—we are called to choose freedom over a childlike obedience, to choose the intricacies and difficulties of work and sexual life over childhood's playful simulations of both, to choose conflict over harmony, and to journey out into the world despite our intense longing to remain home and to forfeit our adulthood. If we affirm our adulthood and think about ourselves, not just Adam and Eve, as having eaten of the forbidden fruit, then we may come to appropriate both our sexuality and our work life not simply as a curse but in their full, often conflicting dimensions. A curse on work and sexuality hovers over our remembrance of a garden of good love and good work. We have to deal with both traditions. It does not help us to pronounce the world inside the orchard "obedient" and the hostile world of the wilderness "disobedient." Orthodoxy is reactionary not only because it portrays our real lives as adult workers and lovers in the tradition of the curse, but also because it nourishes our regressive dream of crawling back into the womb and returning to the garden once more. All too often Christianity has offered us an understanding of reality shaped by the curse, on the one hand, and the promise of escape, on the other, the ever-illusive dream of quitting, going home, never growing up.

A fresh understanding of the two biblical traditions of the garden and the wilderness may lead us to a new and better synthesis than the one afforded by the concepts of obedience and disobedience, which further entrenches an authoritarian understanding of the relationship between God and human beings. How can we live under the curse that casts a pall of futility over our work and sexual lives and at the same time retain the memory of paradise and a different vision, not just as a stored fragment from our metaphysical past but as a vital force contributing to the shape of our future as well? To appreciate our createdness is to remember our life in Eden; it means being able to work and to love while striving for the realization of our oldest common dream under the conditions of a curse that are renewed again and again. The paradise and curse traditions become meaningless if we separate them from each other. Embracing the image of paradise without appreciating the reality of the curse amounts to a nostalgic and sentimental longing for childhood. But isolating the curse from remembrance and the promise of paradise serves to legitimate the status quo. The curse then lives on in its secularized manifestations. The powers-that-be continue to proclaim their commandment: Thou shalt not love but make war against your neighbor; thou shalt not work for the common good but kill yourself in meaningless work.

The symbolism of the garden, the orchard, the oasis keeps the dream of good work alive—"good" meaning fruitful, enjoyable, rewarding work. It is a heresy to consider the Fall as the absolute destruction of the human being and her capacities, human work, and human sexuality. It is perhaps an overly Protestant heresy to understand the Fall as the ultimate devastation of the goodness of humankind and the rest of creation. The story of the Fall conveys an understanding of the human being as fallen but not absolutely destroyed. Neither work nor our capacities for love and work are absolutely destroyed by virtue of the Fall.

Creation continued after the Fall, and it still exists today. In the Garden of Eden, Adam and Eve left behind a phase of their existences; they did not undo creation.

Theologically we are trained to separate God's creation from human work. We do not see the relation between God and the worker mediated through work. As a young student of theology, I had a very different understanding of God's creation. There was a time when I could not think of myself as a co-creator or as a partner of God. I had failed to perceive the relation between God and the worker. And I think my blindness was due to the bourgeois world view that primarily relates work to money and not to creation. When we think about work, the first thing that usually comes to mind is money. We may never completely fathom the extent to which we have been brainwashed by our bourgeois upbringing and education; we may never cease to be surprised by the "little bourgeois" in ourselves. The bourgeois in myself was the one who had never before made the connection between work and creation. For a long time I had separated creation from my own life. I had pondered creation in a purely aesthetic way, never in terms of my life and work. The theology of the bourgeoisie deals with work under the themes of curse and hardship. The secular ideology obstructs the emergence of a different theology of work in its reduction of the value of work to the pursuit of cold cash.

One of the basic characteristics of bourgeois societies is the split between the private and public realms. Although labor itself falls within the public domain, selling yourself in the job market is your private affair, just as securing cheap labor is the private problem of the manufacturer. Likewise, salaries are negotiated as a private contract between two seemingly equal parties, one of whom, in fact, as the owner of the means of production, has absolute power over the other. Once labor was separated from shared social goals and from the control of common citizens' organizations during the early bourgeois epoch, its meaning progressively deteriorated. We still observe this process at work today in our neighborhoods as the corner grocer, the local butcher, and the baker are replaced by the large supermarket chain. Some of the older forms of labor are still vital in Europe, but they are gradually dying out as Europeans become more and more involved in monopolistic capitalism. Our experience of work is increasingly one of futility and meaning-lessness because we value work only as a means of acquiring more things.

We have stripped the dignity from the human as a worker. We define what the worker does by virtue of the amount of money he or she receives for services rendered. We circumscribe his freedom. Ironically, freedom ends at the gates of the factory. Liberal ideology detests dicta-torship as a form of government yet tolerates it in the workplace. The owners of a plant may decide to move an entire work force of several thousand people or to fire them in pursuit of cheaper labor without ever consulting the people whose lives have been completely uprooted by this dictatorial decision. This is what we call free enterprise. On plant closings, the Western International Conference on Economic Dis-location says:

> It is a classic case of profits (for someone else) taking priority over the lives of people. Sometimes, ironically, the plant is showing a profit, but not a large enough one to satisfy the stockholders. So it is dismantled as a tax write-off, its equipment sold for whatever the market will bring, and the corporation either "diversifies" or relocates the plant in another part of the country where labor is unorganized and wages are lower, or overseas, where the corporation has received advance guarantees that there will be no "unrest," meaning that any move to organize workers or establish a union will be immediately suppressed.[5]

Increasingly workers across the globe are the victims of management decisions to which they are not party and which leave them vulnerable to unemployment, economic exploitation, and sooner or later utter des-titution.

A contrast to this scenario is the positive understanding of the human being as a worker and of the role of work as co-creative action, as soli-darity, which is present in many of today's liberation movements. The Christian Workers Fellowship in Sri Lanka, for example, has written a workers' mass that implies a different theology of work.[6] The first part, when the traditional oil lamp is kindled while people sing, is called "Awareness": "Burn out our easy willingness to conform / To comfor-table patterns of right and wrong / To set up one man's profit and an-other's harm. / Light our burdened conscience, keep our wills strong."

The second part of the liturgy is a confession called "Self-Criticism." It says:

> Let us then, comrades, identify all that mars this unity and undermines our brotherhood:
>
> Our acquiescence in the exploitation of man by man;
> Our toleration of social oppression of all kinds;
> Our acceptance of unfair discrimination based on race, caste, creed, class;
> Let us recall how we have let each other down and dodged the truth about ourselves.

In simple language this workers' mass talks about what is different in the liberation congregation or the liberation community. The traditional intercession, called "Orientation," illustrates the difference:

> We pray for all oppressors,
> the imperialists, the capitalists, the bureaucrats,
> that they may be disarmed and overcome by the power of people's solidarity and love.

> We seek to commit ourselves to the struggle for liberation unreservedly.
> We seek to change our lives and to change the structure of our society.
> We seek a revolution of mind and spirit,
> a revolution social, economic, political,
> an unceasing revolution in human relationships.

> Land to the tillers,
> Factories to the workers,
> Leading to the realization of power by the working people in the interests of all,
> In order to help build a new society,
> a new man,
> a new heaven,
> and a new earth.

Theology continues to move forward today—liberation theologies specifically—by means of new liturgies coming out of the struggle that workers wage for a new identity. New liturgies emerge from their struggle for justice. The struggle itself is a means of overcoming both oppression and the repressive side of a religious tradition that has had no room for the identity of the working people.

We are at a point in the history of Christianity when we must begin anew by spelling out our theology in relation to the human being, to our sexuality, to our work, and to war and peace, in light of the gospel's liberating power. To this end, liberation theology has taught us something valuable in terms of hermeneutics, namely, to distinguish between the repressive and liberating traditions in Christianity. Only when we are able to ferret out and to scrutinize critically the repressive and liberating strains in Christian teaching will we be able to move beyond doctrinaire, authoritarian approaches to biblical pronouncement. I find myself in greatest conflict with fundamentalist Christians who subscribe fiercely to scriptural inerrancy, forsaking the distinction between the repressive and the liberating traditions which is so vivid in the biblical teaching on work.

The "curse tradition," which views labor as punishment for the Fall, is what I would call the repressive tradition in Christianity: "Cursed is the ground because of you; in toil you shall eat of it all the days of your life; thorns and thistles it shall bring forth to you" (Gen. 3:17). This text tells us that before the Fall nature gave forth freely of its bounty to humanity. Thorns and thistles are symbols of the hostility that arose between humanity and nature as a result of the Fall. Although necessary for survival, labor thus came to connote God's punishment for human sin, precluding any notion of human fulfillment, creativity, or joy in work. Just as there are in the Bible numerous examples of this repressive tradition, so there are also numerous illustrations of what I would call the liberating tradition, in which work is portrayed not as a means of survival in a hostile environment but as an expression of our being created in God's image. In a liberating perspective, work has to do with life and not simply with survival.

Perhaps the most exquisite and telling image for a liberating understanding of the human task is the image of the vineyard and its gardeners which appears throughout the Scriptures (Mic. 4:4 and Isa. 5:1ff.). It is not accidental that the image of the vineyard, rooted as it is in the ethos of collective human labor (we have to do this together, otherwise it will not work), is also used as a metaphor for relationship, specifically the bond between the lover and the beloved. The Song of Solomon, for example, begins with the enticing poem of a young woman who was made "keeper of the vineyards." The work she is ordered to perform becomes intertwined with sexual play; her poem abounds with erotic allusions. "My own vineyard I have not kept!" (1:6) she exclaims, because her lover, as she sees it, is the keeper of her vineyard. She bids her lover to come to her in the fields:

> Let us go out early to the vineyards,
>   and see whether the vines have budded,
> whether the grape blossoms have opened
>   and the pomegranates are in bloom.
> There I will give you my love.
>   (Song of Sol. 7:12)

The image of the vineyard in the Song of Solomon stands for erotic pleasure and lovemaking. This image also functions in the Bible as a symbol of peace in the abiding relationship between Israel and its God (Isa. 5:1) and as a symbol of economic justice, looking to the time when the planters shall enjoy the fruit of the vine and the oppressors shall be driven away (Jer. 31:5; Isa. 27:2; 55:1). There are actually three dimensions to this image, which provide us with a humanizing, liberating theology of work. The three dimensions are self-expression, contribution to or relatedness to society, and reconciliation with nature through work. To be created in God's image means growing into these most fundamental dimensions of human existence. It means becoming co-creators through work and love.

NOTES

1. See Donna Day-Lower, "Reworking the Work Ethic," *The Other Side* 19, no. 6 (June 1983): 11.

2. Phyllis Trible, *God and the Rhetoric of Sexuality* (Philadelphia: Fortress Press, 1978), p. 85.

3. Ibid.

4. Abraham Heschel, *Between God and Man: An Interpretation of Judaism* (New York: The Free Press, 1959), p. 221.

5. Robert McAfee Brown, Ignacio Castuera, Richard W. Gillett, and Faith Annette Sand, "Community or Chaos? A Pastoral Letter and Call to Action," issued by the Western International Conference on Economic Dislocation, Los Angeles, California, February 1982.

6. "Workers' Mass," published by the Christian Workers Fellowship in Sri Lanka.

7

Work as self-expression

Several years ago I discovered the meaning of work when I contacted the teacher of my youngest child, then a first-grader at an excellent school in Manhattan. One day I became impatient with my daughter's progress at school. They had not yet taught her, at age six, to read or write. So I visited her teacher to ask when the children would start to work. "Work!" he scoffed. "What do you mean? You're talking about work! Can't you see what's going on here? Don't you see that these strong workers, these children, are building a town with their blocks?" He sent me home with this response, a response I was to mull over and benefit from in the ensuing years. His response changed my mind, moving me from a myopic, production-oriented perspective on work to a more humane understanding of work. I discovered the meaning of work in its three essential dimensions: self-expression, social-relatedness, and reconciliation with nature by way of this experience.

These three dimensions of human labor are spiritual as well as material. The spiritual dimension of work is all too easily overlooked. When I questioned the teacher about my child's progress, for example, I displayed a spiritually impoverished perspective on work. Here I attempt to take the flesh-and-blood human being seriously as a worker who realizes God's image through work. E. F. Schumacher, to whom I am greatly indebted, observes in his *Good Work* that "the question of what work does to the worker is hardly ever asked."[1] This is true. It was certainly true of me as a mother six years ago. I was not thinking about what work did to the worker, even to the elementary-school worker, and yet how the work affects the worker is a most important question. If we neglect this question, we will restrict human work to one purpose only, namely, to provide necessary, useful goods and services—as if that could be accomplished without reflecting on the author of work, the worker. The biblical creation narrative teaches us, as other religious and wisdom traditions do, that the purposeful activity of producing is linked to the human striving for perfection. Work enables "every one of us to use and thereby perfect our gifts like good stewards."[2] Schumacher recovers for us the dignity of the worker, or the steward, and the yearning for self-perfection and creativity that underlies human activity. If we understand life as a school, a training ground in which we strive to become something more than we are at present, then work becomes creative praxis.

Good work gives the person a chance to utilize and to develop her faculties. We have to learn "to reject meaningless, boring, stultifying, or nerve-wracking work," as Schumacher maintains, "in which a man (or a woman) is made the servant of a machine or a system."[3] I concur with Schumacher that it is extremely important to teach people to reject unsatisfying, pointless, or nerve-wracking work. Work should be a joy in our lives, and it is crucial for our attainment of full personhood. Thomas Aquinas said that there can be no joy in life without joy in work. The opposite of this joy in medieval philosophy is laziness, or *acedia*, the meaning of which is closer to depression, listlessness, lack of energy, malaise, and laziness in a more existential sense than the word in English conveys. *Acedia* was a severe problem among the cloistered monks and nuns of medieval society, where it was considered to be a sign of the "sadness of the soul" bereft of joy and energy. If we never experience the joy of life in our work, we never mature as full persons. We must not settle for less than work that is good for the worker. We need work for our development, for the perfection of our souls.

Unfortunately, most forms of work are utterly unsatisfying, boring, and meaningless:

> Mechanical, artificial, divorced from nature, utilizing only the smallest part of man's potential capabilities, it [work] sentences the great majority of workers to spending their lives in a way which contains no worthy challenge, no stimulus to self-perfection, no chance of development, no element of Beauty, Truth, or Goodness.[4]

Look for these elements in our work. Where are they? A contemporary of Marx stated that "the subdivision of labor is the assassination of a people."[5] The subdivision of labor is a direct attack on the element of beauty, truth, or goodness in work. The extreme forms of labor division are all destructive to our potentials in that they make only partial use of them. In understanding what good work means and what it does to the worker, the paradigm of the artist is most relevant. There is an element of art in good work. Art, like all good work, enables us to release the power of our imaginations and to become persons as we use this power to come up with an invention, a new solution to a problem, a new way of working. In this sense, the worker-artist collaborates with God in creating, and she or he experiences this labor, praxis, self-activity as pleasure and enjoyment. Art pleases the intellect and the senses, and so does good work.

The vision of self-expression and self-fulfillment in work is more than a utopian dream of people who suffer under the curse tradition of meaningless work. A theology of work must have a visionary, prophetic, or utopian element. As the Book of Proverbs says, "Where there is no vision, the people perish" (29:18, KJV). If there are both repressive and liberating traditions in Christianity, the task of theology is to uncover, to unmask, to critique the repressive tradition and to reveal the true meaning of human work and the identity of its agent, the worker. Good work is a basic human need. We destroy the human being if work means functioning without joy, without fulfillment, without imagination. If we labor under this curse tradition, then we have to recall for ourselves that fulfilling work is a human need. We need to understand ourselves as co-creators who require constructive and joyful work in which we are challenged to develop our creative potential.

The sense of wholeness implied in the concept of good work as a basic human need is marred especially by the division of labor we experience from early childhood onward. As every adequate critique of culture maintains, modern education has produced a variety of specialists who, in common parlance, know more and more about less and less. One result of this intellectual and emotional underdevelopment is "the inability of the person to develop self-government and to interact critically with the surrounding social order."[6] The depoliticization of society is a grave consequence of unfulfilling work in which no self-expression is permitted. People are trained to use such a miniscule part of their brains, such a limited range of their capacities, that their potentials never reach fruition. If at a certain point they are given the opportunity to move beyond these confines, people often fail, as was the case in Yugoslavia for a time. The capitalist countries watched what turned out to be a long experiment in Yugoslavian worker self-governance and just gloated. "We always told you that workers were unable to manage a factory" was the gist of their rebuff as the new Yugoslavian system of worker self-governance indeed catapulted into mismanagement, the bankruptcy of factories, and corruption. This was hardly surprising inasmuch as mismanagement, bankruptcy, and corruption had plagued the Yugoslavian capitalist system for centuries. It took considerable time and effort before the new class of self-ruled workers learned how to use freedom responsibly and to combine the economic goal of high productivity with the social goal of enhancing the dignity of workers through self-government. Although beset with problems, the Yugoslavian experiment is now functioning. It represents one of the most important workers' experiments based on a democratic understanding of self-rule and management in our time.

Schumacher aptly summarizes what young, rebellious people would say about work and their hopes for meaningful work:

> I don't want to join the rat race. Not be enslaved by machines, bureaucracies, boredom, ugliness. I don't want to become a moron, robot, commuter. . . . I want to deal with people, not masks. People matter. Nature matters. Beauty matters. Wholeness matters. I want to be able to *care*.[7]

This is a beautiful summary of how most people actually feel. It is the intent of the Green party in West Germany, for example, to forge a program that will overcome meaningless work in favor of a wholistic understanding of work which in turn will retard and impede the death of human creativity we experience in industrial society. The same aspiration has been articulated in the works of utopian socialists, the prescientific socialists before Marx such as Fourier, Proudhon, Weitling, and others, who envisioned a society in which the inequitable division of labor would not exist and people would find fulfillment in their work.

Another dream for the emergence of meaningful work was embodied in the Catholic Worker movement, which strongly emphasized labor as a free gift rather than as a commodity to be bought and sold. In his *Easy Essays*, the self-taught philosopher Peter Maurin (1877–1949), whom Dorothy Day called "a genius, a saint, an agitator, a writer, a lecturer, a poor man, and a shabby tramp, all in one,"[8] envisioned a society "based on creed instead of greed" and voluntary poverty. He proposed a "green revolution," in which unemployed people would become self-employed working the land, and rooted as he was in the personalist philosophy of traditional Catholicism, he inveighed against the dehumanizing effects of industrialized labor:

> Carlyle says:
> "He who has found his work
> let him look for no other blessedness."
> But workmen
> cannot find happiness
> in mechanized work.
> As Charles Devas says:
> "The great majority having to perform
> some mechanized operation
> which requires little thought
> and allows no originality
> and which concerns an object
> in the transformation of which,
> whether previous or subsequent,
> they have no part,
> cannot take pleasure in their work."
> Eric Gill says:
> "The notion of work has been separated
> from the notion of art.
> The notion of useful has been separated
> from the notion of beautiful.
> The artist, that is to say,
> the responsible workman,
> has been separated from all other workmen.
> The factory hand
> has no responsibility for what he produces.
> He has been reduced to a sub-human condition
> of intellectual irresponsibility.
> Industrialism has released the artist
> from the necessity of making anything useful.
> Industrialism has also released the workman
> from making anything amusing."[9]

As co-founders of the Catholic Worker movement, Peter Maurin and Dorothy Day shared a unique vision of how the Christian tradition could contribute to a thoroughly new understanding of work. They claimed that "labor was related to thought and that thought was not a commodity but a spiritual faculty."[10] Every worker in his or her work must be related to thought and should be taught to think. The Friday night meetings of the Catholic Worker brought together "educational workers" or "cultural workers" (as I would call myself) and production workers for the purpose of "clarifying" their thinking and their roles in order to achieve shared goals. These people had learned to channel their freedom away from the acquisitive society by keeping in mind "that means had to harmonize with the ultimate ends pursued."[11]

If one is part of an acquisitive society, one tends to think of work as neutral, because only the end matters, not the means. The end is money, so people think about money and work for more of it. The end eventually defines everything, and the importance of the means recedes. This philosophical system is a travesty, because when consideration of means is discarded our relationships to one another and to the earth degenerate. One of the strong claims in the philosophy of nonviolence is that the means change the ends. This is true for the workplace. Good work must therefore be understood as an end in itself and not just as a means to get something else.

What does work do to the worker? If we overlook this question, we are doomed to understand work only in terms of its exchange value and thereby to destroy the self-expression of the worker. There is strong support for a personalistic approach to work in an encyclical letter of Pope John Paul II, *Laborem exercens*, which provides insights into a new theology of work.[12] Emerging from the philosophical tradition of Christian personalism represented by such thinkers as Jacques Maritain, Emmanuel Mounier, and the Russian exile Nikolai Berdyaev, John Paul here extends the principles of a Christian understanding of the person to the realm of labor. The pope's emphasis on the subjectivity of the worker, grounded in her having been made in the image of God, is the point of departure for critiquing both capitalism and state socialism as systems that deny the dignity of the worker in her work. "Human subjectivity is the locus of divine presence."[13] This is the deepest reason for the priority of labor over capital. And the subjectivity of the worker, the need for self-expression, responsibility, and creativity, cannot be taken away from her even under alienating conditions.

Despite alienating work, the human being remains a subject and never totally becomes an object. One strength of the encyclical is its emphasis on human dignity even under debasing conditions. Created in the image of God, the worker cannot wholly lose his subjectivity. We should reflect on this aspect of *Laborem exercens* in light of the Polish workers' movement in the 1980s and the struggle of "Solidarity" against state socialism. The principle of the "priority of labor over capital" applies to state socialism as well as to advanced capitalism and provides a tool for radical criticism of both systems. New forms of cooperative ownership and cooperative management in a decentralized democratic form of socialism are envisioned and partially realized in the Yugoslavian model of socialism. The papal encyclical is critical of those trends in Marx and Marxism that define the human being as an assemblage of social relations and forces, without understanding the power of the subjects which transcends a merely positivistic view of the human historical project. It is wrong to define human beings solely by the forces of production and the social relations determined by these modes. To define humanity in this way is to overlook that God is redemptively at work in present history and calls people to struggle against those powers that constrict and violate humanity.

The encyclical starts with the human person, who "is made in the visible universe an image and likeness of God . . . and . . . is placed in it in order to subdue the earth. From the beginning therefore he is called to work."[14] The theological foundation of the encyclical is the understanding of the human being as a worker. God has created people to be creators and to realize their humanity through work. The human being actualizes herself, becomes the subject she is meant to be, becomes truly herself, through work. In good work, we discover who we are, we assume responsibility for ourselves and others, and we lay the foundations for our own future and society's future.

The encyclical draws a helpful distinction between the subjective and the objective sides of labor. The objective side refers to the product of labor; it signifies not only the goods produced by the worker, but also the machines and technology used for their production. Technology, according to the pope, should be our ally:

It facilitates . . . work, perfects, accelerates, and augments it. It leads to an increase in the quantity of things produced by work and in many cases improves their quality. However it is also a fact that in some instances technology can cease to be man's ally and become almost his enemy, as when the mechanization of work "supplants" him, taking away all personal satisfaction and the incentive to creativity and responsibility, when it deprives many workers of their previous employment or when, through exalting the machine, it reduces man to the status of its slave.[15]

In this sense, the objective side of labor has its own dialectic: it can be either an ally of the worker or an enemy.

Because work is never to be understood simply in its objective sense, the encyclical clarifies what work does to the worker. The pope speaks about the "gospel of work," which is given implicitly in "the fact that the one who, while being God, became like us in all things devoted most of the years of his life on earth to manual work at the carpenter's bench."[16] Whereas the ancient world considered manual work unworthy of free men and therefore the lot of slaves, Christianity "brought about a fundamental change of ideas in this field."[17] When God, incarnate in Jesus, became a worker, our understanding of work was finally freed from the tradition of the curse. The new dignity of the worker appears in this gospel of work. The encyclical states:

> The basis for determining the value of human work is not primarily the kind of work being done, but the fact that the one who is doing it is a person. The sources of the dignity of work are to be sought primarily in the subjective dimension, not in the objective one.[18]

The distinction between the subjective and the objective sides of labor is neither value-free nor merely descriptive. It gives priority to what work does to the worker not to what her work produces. Responsibility and self-realization are of greater value and importance than the commodities produced.

Out of this revaluation of the subjective meaning of work over its objective goals follows another principle, namely, the priority of labor over capital. These principles, the priority of the subjective side of labor over its objective side and the priority of labor over capital, are interdependent. In a capitalist economy, labor is seen from its objective side alone (as I saw the "labor" of my first-grade daughter). The worker is treated as an object and thus easily experiences herself as the object of the machinery, the product, and the industrial process. Workers lose the sense of being subjects and agents of their own lives. Capital achieves priority over human life. But "justice means that capital is made to serve labor."[19]

We humans have an undeniable need for self-expression. Labor, in its subjective dimension, is a way to fulfill this need. Because the Christian faith is not neutral to essential human needs, Christians must claim work as the self-expression of the worker. Saying that God is already redemptively at work in present history is a statement of faith in the human project as willed by the source of life, even if the objective conditions seem hopeless. To claim God as the source of our co-creative power as workers moves us beyond determinism. God and the claim of an absolute human dignity are interdependent.

NOTES

1. E. F. Schumacher, *Good Work* (New York: Harper & Row, 1979), p. 3.
2. Ibid.
3. Ibid., p. 119.
4. Ibid., p. 27.
5. Ibid., p. 42.
6. Marc H. Ellis, *Peter Maurin: Prophet in the Twentieth Century* (New York and Toronto: Paulist Press, 1981), p. 106.
7. Schumacher, *Good Work*, p. 50.
8. William D. Miller, *Dorothy Day: A Biography* (New York: Harper & Row, 1982), p. 228.
9. Peter Maurin, *Easy Essays*, essays selected and reprinted from the *Catholic Worker* by the people at the Catholic Worker Farm, West Hamlin, Virginia, 1974.
10. Ellis, *Maurin*, p. 114.
11. Ibid.
12. Pope John Paul II, *Laborem exercens*, as printed in *The Priority of Labor: A Commentary on "Laborem Exercens," Encyclical Letter of Pope John Paul II*, by Gregory Baum (New York and Toronto: Paulist Press, 1982), pp. 93–152. It should be noted that the moral viability of the papal analysis of work is undermined by its blatant sexism. The encyclical refers to human beings exclusively as men and to work almost entirely in terms of the male labor force. The pope's understanding of the social role of women is clear: Their province is the family. Sexist, even misogynist, statements from the Vatican are historical commonplaces. The importance of *Laborem exercens* lies in its progressive vision of hu-

man work, a vision that will ultimately prove to be subversive of the global domination of women. The pope's emphasis on the creative, self-realizing aspect of human labor stands in direct contradiction to his rigid conservatism where sex roles are concerned.

13. Gregory Baum, *The Priority of Labor: A Commentary on "Laborem Exercens," Encyclical Letter of Pope John Paul II* (New York and Toronto: Paulist Press, 1982), p. 17.

14. *Laborem exercens*, p. 95.

15. Ibid., pp. 103–4.

16. Ibid., p. 105.

17. Ibid.

18. Ibid., pp. 105–6.

19. Baum, *Priority of Labor*, p. 30.

8

Work and social-relatedness

The second essential element of good work pertains to its societal dimension. Work is the activity that relates a person to her society. Work creates community and imbues people with the pride of belonging to a group dedicated to pursuits both respected and needed by society. Work is a communal enterprise. Even the work we think of as solitary and lonely, like the work of the artist or the scientist, is conditioned and motivated by society. And art or science is qualitatively better when its communal commission is recognized by the cultural worker. I do not subscribe to the glorification of the solitary artist who answers only to the muse within. The artist who is deeply involved in the lives of others forges a link between art and human needs, rejecting the ideology of art for art's sake or art for the artist's sake. We desperately need artists and cultural workers who are accountable to their societies.

If the first question we must ask about work is what it does to the worker, the second question we must ask is what work does to the community. How does work relate the working person to the community? This question, like the previous one, calls for a response that is simultaneously materialistic and spiritual. Our response must be materialistic, because it must encompass such things as compensation for work, the organization of labor, the planning and imaginative components of work, and the usefulness of any enterprise for the community. But because these technological, social, and political facets of human work must also be examined with the conviction that labor has priority over capital and that people matter, our response must also be a spiritual one.

To ask what work does to the worker and to the community is to do more than pose a technical question, the answer to which is a better, more streamlined, more efficient means of production. Because work mediates our relations to others, it should epitomize our relatedness. If we participate in creation and imitate God through our work, then our creation is also a sign of our relatedness and shared existence. Through work that is true to who we are, we share in the work of creation and enter into a continuous process of giving and taking, teaching and learning that characterizes all good work. Yet work in Western industrialized societies entails, overwhelmingly, competition against, not relation to, others.

One of the complaints frequently voiced by older workers in highly technological workplaces is that they have lost the role of teacher. Loss of their teaching role has left a void that is experienced as an assault on their dignity. To grow old without having anything to offer younger people, to lose the right to give something out of one's experience, is a crippling blow to one's dignity and sense of self. Part of our work involves communicating our experience—the work stored in our minds, our hearts, and our hands—to other people, not just hoarding it for ourselves. Today's workers are finding themselves expendable, their experience discarded in the wake of technological change that has rendered their knowledge obsolete. What they have learned is assumed to have no value for the next generation. Therefore, the giving and receiving, the teaching and learning processes that are essential to good work —the exchange that goes beyond productivity strictly defined—are destroyed when the pace of technological change outdistances the human ability to respond to change.

All workers act within a particular society and culture. All have inherited tools, technology, and knowledge from past generations of workers. They stand on the shoulders of earlier generations. By educating workers and society about past forms of work, we deepen our respect for the legacy of our working ancestors. To develop a historical sense of what work has been, to know what our grandparents did and the path they took to their achievements, is the aim of an educational process that puts self-understanding and human worth before capital. Yet this approach to work is almost unheard of in a nation like the United States, which evaluates labor primarily in terms of productivity. Respect for the worker and past workers, however, is essential to a communal understanding of work and in the long run to productivity as well. Work is communal not only in the space of a given community but also in time, as the shared memory of what we have received from the past that accompanies us into the future.

We must produce in order to survive, and in order to survive we must produce together. Our essential neediness and our relatedness, or the communality of our existence, are inextricably linked. We cannot produce what we need to sustain our livelihood apart from each other. Karl Marx offers an enlightened vision of the kind of relationships we could have with one another and the entire human race through our productivity:

> Supposing that we had produced in a human manner; each of us would in his production have doubly affirmed himself and his fellow man. I would have: (1) objectified in my production my individuality and its peculiarity and thus both in my activity enjoyed an individual expression of my life and also in looking at the object have had the individual pleasure of realizing that my personality was objective, visible to the senses and thus a power raised beyond all doubt. (2) In your enjoyment or use of my product I would have had the direct enjoyment of realizing that I had both satisfied a human need by my work and also objectified the human essence and therefore fashioned for another human being the object that met his need. (3) I would have been for you the mediator between you and the species and thus been acknowledged and felt by you as a completion of your own essence and a necessary part of yourself and have thus realized that I am confirmed both in your thought and in your love. In my expression of my life I would have fashioned your expression of your life, and thus in my own activity have realized my own essence, my human, my communal essense.[1]

The three elements in Marx's vision of how a fully human life could be are similar to the three dimensions of good work that I attempt to identify in this book. Producing in a "human manner," for Marx, leads to the "individual expression" of one's life, the satisfaction of a human need, and the realization of the human, communal essence of the species. Contrary to the common prejudice, I do not find anything narrow, reductionistic, or merely economistic in this vision of human production. Instead Marx's vision of work stands in continuity with the prophetic biblical tradition of justice and fulfillment (*shalom*) for everyone.

If we look for evidence of atheism in Marx's vision of human production, the only thing we can pinpoint is the absence of a divine agent in bringing a human manner of production into being. However, in my opinion, belief in an otherworldly divine agent is not a criterion of Christian faith. There are many people who say "Lord, Lord," addressing themselves to a supreme being, but who fail to do the will of God (Matt. 7:21). The true criterion of faith is our being empowered to love and to do justice. To believe in the goodness of creation means believing that we are created to realize together our human, communal essence through work. Far from mirroring a lack of faith, Marx's words attest to his having gone further than most Christians ever do in embracing the possibility of the life abundant which Christ proclaimed.

If we understand creation as stemming from God's desire for relatedness or God's wish to share the earth with the human being, then it follows that work is the place where relatedness, mutuality, and interdependency become visible. In good work, we participate in the flow of teaching and learning, of making our contributions and receiving the contributions of others, of being needed and having our needs met. Good work makes our relatedness visible to ourselves and enhances it. Schumacher maintains that one goal of good work is "to liberate ourselves from our inborn egocentricity," from which we free ourselves "in service to, and in cooperation with, others."[2] When this happens, the "old ego" disappears; Hegel called this phenomenon externalization (*entäusserung*), and he considered it the positive side of alienation.

We can learn much from children about this phenomenon. One of the most misguided things a parent can do is to interrupt a young child immersed in an activity. When children are genuinely absorbed in a task, they display an intense love for work. Children can teach us about what respect for the worker means, namely, honoring the forgetfulness of self that occurs during concentrated periods of good work, and the human need to finish the task at hand. Immersed in good work, we forget time and space, even hunger and thirst. Immersed in good work, our "inborn egocentricity" vanishes, and in its wake the divine self within us is set free. Our energies, no longer hamstrung by egocentricity and the dividedness of self that stifles our potentialities, flow freely and creatively. Good work releases the divine element in us by which we rediscover the source of our creativity and our connection to all living things.

Cooperation in good work generates an enthusiasm that is rooted in a heightened sense of our relatedness to one another. I have experienced this sense of relatedness in small collectives where we produced papers and journals, sharing the work from the idea stage to the final typesetting. In such groups I discovered that creativity can be shared and the labor division overcome in a process of mutual give-and-take. There were, of course, temporary divisions of labor, because it is impossible in any group for everyone to share equally in what are often simultaneous tasks. The collectives in which I worked were different in that the division of labor was established by mutual consensus and was flexible. The danger in dividing labor lies in our continuing to foster permanent divisions of labor and role definitions to which people are assigned on the basis of race, class, or sex. We are in dire need of a system that requires us to share the alienated labor, the unenjoyable, non-self-enriching tasks that accompany any human undertaking. To this end, the Chinese during the "cultural revolution" created a fluid division of labor. Everyone was expected to do "alienated labor" at one time or another, but no one was expected to do it exclusively and forever. No one was to be excluded from opportunities for learning and continuing education on the basis of sex, age, or social position. A fluctuating division of labor brought business managers and professors to the rice fields and farm women to the classroom. Relatedness to others became visible in the self-organization of large rural communes. The dignity of the worker was restored through such measures, and it is important for us to recall them even though they were abandoned at a later phase of the Chinese revolution.

Instead of experiencing happiness in a profound sense of relatedness, more and more people in Western societies flounder in an emotional wasteland because of the way work is organized. Today the sense of unrelatedness among workers is mounting because of the ever-present threat of losing one's job. Interviews with the unemployed indicate that joblessness is experienced as a form of excommunication. Workers lose not only their jobs but also their channels of communication with the larger society as well. Unemployment results in exclusion from the working community. The current dearth of paid work is bringing about the disintegration of human beings. The sense of relatedness to others among the jobless, no longer grounded in working relationships, grows tenuous or even disappears. The self-worth of the jobless crumbles. Many succumb to alcoholism, suicide, and mental illness. Kurt Vonnegut's *Player Piano* chronicles the despair of the average man and woman who have no access to work at all in his nightmarish, Orwellian vision of a future society dominated by computers. *Player Piano* unfolds a world in which the educated upper class does the necessary brain work to maintain a system that, having successfully fed, clothed, and housed its citizens, can do nothing to alleviate the spiritual void, the rampant feelings of uselessness, in its population. And as one of the novel's dissident voices concludes:

> Sooner or later someone's going to catch the imagination of these people with some new magic. At the bottom of it will be a promise of regaining the feeling of participation, the feeling of being needed on earth—hell, *dignity*. The police are bright enough to look for people like that, and lock them up under the antisabotage laws.[3]

Vonnegut's vision, written in 1952, has meanwhile become partially true.

Murray H. Finley, president of the Amalgamated Clothing Workers of America and Co-Chairperson of the National Committee for Full Employment, has this to say about high unemployment:

> To the degree that a nation tolerates high unemployment, it loses some of its soul and moral character. Our nation loses its decency when it allows inhumane and irresponsible charts and theories to prevent people from sharing in its economy and the general life of the community.[4]

Finley aptly describes what is happening in the United States at present. More and more workers, even skilled workers, have found their jobs eliminated as a result of the pace of automation and the upsurge in "irresponsible charts and theories" geared to maximizing profits at the expense of people. Meanwhile, the rich fear "invasion" by the poor. According to a report in the *New York Times*, some wealthy towns have taken the extraordinary measure of walling themselves off from the rest of the world.[5] And most of the growing number of communities that have opted for enclosure are not even close to high-crime areas. Walling oneself in is a perfect symbol of the apartheid system required by the wealthy to "protect" themselves from the poor, the jobless, and the so-called unemployable.

As unemployment mounts, work is becoming the focus of discussion in more and more churches. Some people are questioning the meaning of work for the first time. Do we need a new theology of work? Is the Protestant work ethic version of work, especially as it lends itself to workaholism, sufficient, or do we not in fact need a new understanding of work? These are typical queries. Others question the wisdom of probing the nature of good work when the opportunity to have any work at all is at stake. I believe, however, that the issues of good work and unemployment are interrelated. It is essential to raise the issue of good work at a time when people are desperately searching for any work. Our very definition of work as wage labor determines what joblessness means and makes for society's unwillingness to deal with unemployment. There is even a tendency to develop economic theories based on the acceptance of high unemployment. Those too discouraged to continue looking for work are branded "the unemployable," as if their lot were a natural given.

The current global economic crisis should force us to examine what the capitalist, industrial economy has done to workers and to explore alternatives to the prevailing concept of work. In the wealthy, industrialized nations, this crisis manifests itself in technological innovations that make certain forms of labor obsolete and in the proliferation of "runaway shops," a term that refers to the flight of capital and factories to nonunion areas in the United States or to countries where an exploitable work force is guaranteed by military dictatorships. In poor countries, oppressive measures such as censorship of the press, suppression of public dissent, illegal arrests, torture, and disappearances of thousands of citizens have their economic rationale in the maintenance of exploitative working conditions.[6]

We must ask ourselves this: Was not work, as it was designed in capitalist economies, undesirable from the very beginning? Is industrialism not aimed at increasing productivity at the expense of the worker's satisfaction? The idea of "saving labor" alone, which is one of the basic goals of industrial production, implies that work is a curse, something to be gotten rid of. There is no room for the joy, fulfillment, or dignity of the worker in an idea that stamps labor with "the mark of undesirability."[7] From the outset, there was no dignity in most industrial jobs and no concern for social-relatedness in the organization of the workplace.

Capitalism relies on the power of three deadly human sins—greed, envy, and avarice—to stimulate productivity and consumerism. By successfully manipulating the instincts connected to our sense of ownership, capitalism ensures the priority of capital over labor and the destruction of relatedness. An acquisitive society relates work to having, not to being; to owning, not to sharing; to getting, not to growing. By undermining our relatedness, by making it useless, an acquisitive society deadens the desire for good work. If we would view the problem of joblessness as a chance to develop better, more dignified, forms of labor, we might replace ambition and competition with an increased capacity for mutual aid. We might, as Peter Maurin envisioned, "foster a society based on creed instead of greed, on systematic unselfishness, on gentle personalism instead of rugged individualism. . . . [We might] create a new society within the shell of the old."[8] Those who now have no paid occupation would not necessarily be without work if work were to include such things as day care for children, restoring homes, repairing shops, community organizing, developing alternative sources of energy, combating environmental pollution, and creating viable means of public transportation. The countercultural tendency toward "reowning" our schools, medical institutions, transporation systems, and food production through shared, decentralized community efforts may foster a new understanding of work as self-expression, relatedness to society, and reconciliation with nature.

The papal encyclical *Laborem exercens* reflects this new understanding of work in its espousal of two seemingly contradictory social necessities: a planned economy and decentralization of government. There is a need, on the one hand, for government to safeguard workers' rights in the workplace, to create retraining programs that equip workers with skills to perform today's jobs, and to foster an industrial policy that synchronizes production plans with available resources and markets. On the other hand, there is a need for workers to have control over their lives and their productivity at the workbench. The values that underlie these two necessities are justice and solidarity, both of which lie at the heart of a theology of work. "Justice means that capital is made to serve labor," asserts Gregory Baum in his commentary on *Laborem exercens*.[9] Meanwhile, solidarity is the most profound form of relatedness and togetherness that can arise from our work relations. Workers' solidarity with one another and with the unemployed is more worthwhile and more important than the objects they produce. A theology of work accords a higher place to our interrelatedness than to our productivity. To understand ourselves as created in God's image is to see ourselves as co-creators first of all. To participate in the unfinished creation is to choose freely and affirm solidarity with our fellow workers.

In the winter of 1981 the Polish miners in Sosnowiec, Lower Silesia, created a new form of solidarity which they called "active strike." Instead of halting production to demonstrate their grievances or bargaining with the state, these miners occupied their workplace and devised their own system of governance and plan for producing coal. They also elected to turn over part of the coal to a kindergarten, a nursing home, and several farms. The "active strike" was the Polish miners' way of assuming control over the material and productive forces and giving the fruit of their labor to the people. As such, it represented a gift from the Polish workers to the workers of the world. *Solidarnosc* ceased to refer only to a labor organization; it came to mean a new way of living and working together.

NOTES

1. Karl Marx, "Free Human Production," from *Excerpt-Notes of 1844* as translated by David McLellan in *Marx* (London: Fontana Books, 1975), p. 34.

2. E. F. Schumacher, *Good Work* (New York: Harper & Row, 1979), p. 4.

3. Kurt Vonnegut, Jr., *Player Piano* (New York: Delacorte Press/Seymour Lawrence, 1952), p. 82.

4. As quoted in "Humphrey-Hawkins at a Glance," printed by the National Committee for Full Employment, Washington, D.C., 1983.

5. "Some Rich Towns Being Walled Off," *New York Times*, June 27, 1983, p. A-12.

6. See my "Human Rights in Latin America: On the Problem of Political Abductions," in *Of War and Love* by Dorothee Sölle (Maryknoll, N.Y.: Orbis Books, 1983), pp. 106–26.

7. Schumacher, *Good Work*, p. 27.

8. Peter Maurin, *Easy Essays*, essays selected and reprinted from the *Catholic Worker* by the people at the Catholic Worker Farm, West Hamlin, Virginia, 1974.

9. Gregory Baum, *The Priority of Labor: A Commentary on "Laborem Exercens," Encyclical Letter of Pope John Paul II* (New York and Toronto: Paulist Press, 1982), p. 30.

9

Work as reconciliation with nature

Besides the individual dimension of good work (the self-realization and dignity of the worker) and the communal dimension (relatedness and solidarity), there is a third dimension that a theology of work must consider. The third dimension of good work concerns the objective side of labor, which is interrelated with both its subjective and intersubjective aspects. To name this third dimension "nature," as opposed to *materia*, or object, or production, is to invoke a theological framework at the outset. Earlier I associated the objective side of labor exclusively with production and technology to depict the conflict that has arisen between it and the subjective side of labor in the modern world. The conflict, in which our technological needs are pitted against and perpetually overpower human values, is not inevitable. It has much to do with the way we understand technology in the first place—as the means to ensure our survival in a hostile environment, as a necessary exploitation of nature. We must begin to solve the conflict by reconceiving the objective goal of work.

There is another way to see the objective side of labor. The Bible names and blesses it as "the fruits of our labor," which is a telling expression of the bond between human work and nature. Human work is aimed at re-creating the world and transforming it into what Ernst Bloch in his *Principle of Hope* calls "a home that no one has entered" (*etwas, worin noch niemand war: Heimat*). It is through our most humane activities, in work and in love, that we become co-creators of the new earth, the place we may finally call home. The hope for reconciliation with nature through human work amounts to a rejection of the tra-

103

ditional, masculine aspiration to dominate the earth. This hope has arisen anew in the face of today's ecological crisis, which portends the destruction of the earth. Reconciling ourselves with nature through work is one of the great human projects before us.

We must ask ourselves the extent to which our work, and the consumerism that is related to our perception of work, destroys the earth, even threatens to undo creation. We must ask ourselves what our work contributes to the exploitation of unrenewable natural resources; what it does to the human family, especially to the poor; and finally what it lends to the madness of the military machine that devours so much human labor with its plans for our undoing. The same violence threatens both nature and poor, less technologically developed peoples. The creator's commandment to the first human beings to subdue the earth and to have dominion over all living things (Gen. 1:28) has left its fatal mark on Western history. That historically the West has understood the ruthless suppression and in some instances the extermination of so-called primitive peoples as necessary and inevitable shows that it has taken literally the commandment to subdue and to dominate. And it is not coincidental that the West eradicated societies that pursued a life in harmony with nature, and then went on to exploit the earth's natural resources. Today we witness the culmination of Western imperialism against nature in the nuclearization and militarization of the globe. There was a period in history when the subjugation of nature was necessary to the human project, but this orientation has exceeded its usefulness. Nowhere is this more evident than in the suicidal bent of the arms race.

A theology of work must reflect on how our production and distribution of resources affect Third World populations. There can be no reconciliation with nature without simultaneous reconciliation with the poor. For social relatedness to prevail, we need to ground our work in cooperation and mutual aid instead of in competition and the relentless economic war we wage against poor nations. We should not use the word "peace" to characterize the world in which we now live. We are at war. In the war against the poor, fifteen thousand people die daily from starvation and disease, according to the most moderate estimates. We could help put an end to the casualties by redesigning work and the world economy.

If we are to make peace with the poor, we will have to undergo a conversion in the way we use raw materials, organize the workplace, and decide what we will produce. If justice is to prevail in the workplace, labor must have priority over capital. Today the capital-intensive nature of most Western industries, exported worldwide, prevents more and more poor people in Third World countries from making a living in agriculture. By and large, Western research has been devoted to the production of costly, capital-intensive technology rather than to the development of labor-intensive, intermediate, affordable technology.

The requirement for small-scale technology in labor-intensive settings has been sacrificed on the altar of high technology, where the demand for ever-more complex, capital-costly equipment and systems of production prevails. There is a devastating alliance between our neocolonialist economic order, in which the haves control the have-nots through bank loans, protectionism, and price regulations, and technological overdevelopment, which reduces the poor nations in the south to extreme dependence on the rich nations in the north. Technologically dependent, the poor nations find themselves both economically and politically vulnerable to the prerogatives of the rich, industrialized nations. Should a poor society elect to follow its own model of development, should it attempt to determine its life apart from the dictates of a superpower, the rich swiftly descend to "destabilize" it. Liberated Nicaragua is an example. The Nicaraguans are enormously dependent on the United States for equipment and replacement parts. When U.S. antipathy to the Sandinista government leads to a stoppage or delay of imports, whole communications, power, and production networks are endangered. Technological superiority has enabled the rich, industrialized northern nations to condition decisively the economies and cultures of the poor southern nations.

Life in its fullness means bread and work for all, but as Jan Pronk put it at the 1983 General Assembly of the World Council of Churches in Vancouver: "The beginning of the 1980s is characterized by less work and less bread for more people." In 1972 a barrel of oil cost the equivalent of twenty-six kilos of bananas in the Third World. Today that same barrel costs two hundred kilos of bananas. What will rural workers in the year 2000 be getting for their products? Participation in the world market, forced on the poor nations by the industrialized nations, and the destruction of domestic markets are facts of life everywhere in the Third World. This is the silent war of the rich against the poor. In many fertile areas in Latin America, for example, where rice, corn, and beans were once grown for domestic consumption, there are now plantations owned by multinational corporations. The crops raised there are straw-berries and orchids, both intended for export. The local population goes hungry; the children become feebleminded from lack of protein; the elderly die; and young adults flee the countryside. For whom are these strawberries and orchids raised? Who profits from them?[1]

Good work promotes self-sufficiency, not dependency; it is devoted to, not abstracted from, real human needs. Those who come to under-stand the goal of work as fulfilling the needs of their neighbors tend to experience a transformation in their entire approach to work. Such is the case today in Nicaragua, where the enormous labor of teaching and healing undertaken in the literacy and health campaigns is done by vol-unteers. Their work is reminiscent of an old dream within the Roman Catholic tradition that emerged with Francis of Assisi. As already noted, Francis taught that labor ought to be given as a gift. The early Franciscan mendicants offered their labor to small farmers during har-vest time as a gift. We may toss aside this idea as the utopian dream of a few celibates in a preindustrialized setting, but the foolishness of such dreams may actually help us distance ourselves from the presupposi-tions of our own society. We might then look at our own culture from a different angle, subjecting to scrutiny some of the things we take for granted. We might discover that the acquisitive society is not the only vantage point from which to view work and money.

In support of a functional society Thomas Aquinas said, "All goods are necessary, useful, or superfluous." Peter Maurin refashioned this statement to talk about our relationship to property: "What is necessary to us we must keep. What is useful we may keep or we may give it away. What is superfluous belongs to the poor. What we take with us when we die are the things we give away."[2] Maurin's point is not that we should give superfluous things to the poor out of charity. On the con-trary, our superfluous excess belongs to the poor; the poor have a right to it. We have no right to own or use what is superfluous; if we do, it is a crime. In this sense, each bomb we manufacture is a theft from the poor. Each cruise missile we deploy for future use means fewer and fewer tractors for agricultural development. The world expenditure for the arms race, amounting to $550 billion in 1982,[3] is the greatest economic crime ever committed in history.

The same rule of distinction between the necessary and the superfluous, therefore illegitimate, use of goods applies to labor. All work is either necessary, useful, or superfluous. A functional society would distinguish between work that is necessary for our subsistence, work that is useful and may be given to others as a gift, and work that is superfluous, consuming energy and resources that belong to the poor. I am not talking about a preindustrial utopia. I am pointing to the prospect of our overcoming the nationalistic and therefore egoistic limitations of traditional economic theory and practice. The Brandt report about the North-South conflict and the literature about peace are filled with data about how tractors, mobile pharmacies, and agricultural teaching centers could be constructed instead of cruise missiles and other superfluous things. The East-West conflict is exaggerated as a pretext for filling First World coffers; it is around the North-South conflict that we need to reenvision the goals of our production.

Mass production in the interest of death and the plight of the poor are realities that still evoke a sense of guilt and shame in most people. The majority know that there is something intrinsically wrong with a society that manufactures bomb after bomb but does not feed the hungry. To react with guilt and shame to this fundamental contradiction in our social life is normal. Marx called shame a revolutionary emotion; it is revolutionary because it can help us resist the crime of thievery against the poor. But reconciliation with the poor ultimately cannot be achieved apart from a transformation in our patterns of work. What do we want to produce? What do we need? What is the sociopolitical relevance of our work? All who work must ask themselves these basic questions if we are to effect reconciliation with the poor.

Questions about what we shall produce and what we need raise the prior question of who plans and controls productivity. All workers should be involved in this process. The dignity of the human worker is rooted in his or her capacity to think and to plan. The participation of workers in decision-making is necessary not only for workers' self-respect but also for the just use of goods and labor. Good work reconciles us with the poor; if work lacks this dimension, then it still subscribes to the old order of an acquiescent society that has made of work a degraded exercise in profiteering.

Schumacher provides a good example of collective worker owner-ship and decision-making at Scott Bader, a British plastics company. Scott Bader workers established some "self-denying ordinances" in the interest of a high degree of democracy and participation. One of their ordinances concerned the question of how to distribute profits after taxation and reinvestment. All four hundred members of the company chose to set aside for socially worthy purposes half the profits available for distribution: "For every pound that we distribute to ourselves, we set one pound aside for some external noble purpose."[4] Good work in-corporates this kind of ecumenical perspective, without which we live provincially and fail to recognize our indebtedness to the poorest work-ers of the world. Solidarity, as it comes out of the working-class tradi-tion, means that we orient ourselves not just toward those who have work but also toward those who have been robbed of work. Good work entails giving to the poor not out of condescending charity but out of concern for demonstrating our connectedness through a partner-ship that changes both the giver and the receiver. In the case of Scott Bader, the reconciliatory quality of this new relationship was enhanced by the fact that the decision to distribute half the profits to the needy was made by all the workers at the plant.

Another ordinance set by the Scott Bader Company prohibited the sale of any of its products for use in the manufacture of armaments. Work that would achieve reconciliation with nature must uphold non-violence against nature as one of its operating principles. Yet on a glo-bal scale most work is characterized by violence against nature, which is evident in the rapid depletion of the earth's unrenewable deposits of fossil fuels and metals. And there is an intimate connection between this rape of the earth and rampant social violence. Violence against nature, so deeply written into the industrial script, can turn at any moment into violence against human beings. People are trained to destroy nature, so what is to prevent them from unleashing their capacities for destruction against fellow humans? The hostile social climate that passes for our life together is a direct reflection of our hostility toward the earth.

How does our production affect our use of resources? What does it do to the environment? Rarely do we ask these basic questions that reveal how the quality of our work corresponds to the fate of the earth. In industrialized societies the major "force of productivity," to use Marx's term, is science. Almost all human work is dependent on scientific research. But the common belief persists that science is uniquely endowed with the capacity for total mastery of the environment, and if scientific "advances" happen to produce unwanted side effects, we believe that science will deal with these as well. This is the ideology underlying both science and work, which dismisses full-scale violence against nature as a series of manageable side effects. The dumping of poisons in ever-increasing quantities on the earth's surface is just one example of modern-day violence against nature to which science is party. All life is dependent on the thin film around the globe. When violence against the earth is justified as scientific necessity, however, we are encouraged, in the name of scientific neutrality, to view it differently. Far from being neutral, science is part of the problem in the daily war against nature. And the poor, who can least afford this kind of violence, are often its direct recipients. The poor southern nations are the dumping ground for the North's banned pesticides, chemical fertilizers, and pharmaceuticals. They are repeatedly the victims of the North's defoliants and napalm.

Schumacher has identified four major trends in modern technology that have made it possible for the scientific-technological complex to dominate us. They are the trends toward "ever-bigger size, ever-bigger complexity, ever-bigger capital intensity, and ever-bigger violence."[5] The Concorde, for instance, is a gigantic, intricate, inordinately expensive airplane constructed without regard for resource usage or side effects on the environment. It exemplifies these misdirected trends in technology which have a demonic quality. Reformation Europe believed that if the God of creation were abandoned demons would occupy God's former place in the world. This is not unlike the way I view the ascendancy of the ideology of technology. In its omnipotence and neutrality, it has, for me, become the new demon. Technology has replaced the God of creation; it is the surrogate, all-powerful "deity" whose might no one can escape.

In the recent European debate on the arms race, people have often contended that because nuclear weapons are part of our reality we have to live with them. Those who argue along these lines have already sacrificed their reason, compassion, and sense of human freedom to the god of the scientific-technological complex. They have fallen under the spell of science's supposed neutrality, its objective, value-free posture. Neutrality has preempted what we call in the Judeo-Christian tradition "justice." There is no necessity for the god of science to do justice; neutrality is his ultimate value. Therefore this god is inaccessible to our cries and supplications. This god cannot hear the protests of its victims.

The story of the Fall concludes with God's curse on Adam and Eve; they are forced to battle for their survival on an earth that God has turned against them. The modern era has turned this curse upside down. Today it is the unremitting violence of humanity against the earth that brings a curse on the worker. Workers are not consulted about whether they condone destroying nature. The workplace is more like a school for violence than a place where education for benign conduct toward nature might take place. Nevertheless, we must continue to remind ourselves that there are alternatives. Small-scale, labor-intensive technology as opposed to ever-bigger capital-intensive technology, simpler and less expensive tools, and less violation of the natural cycle are not romantic visions but real options that have already been tested in many regions of the world.

A theology of work must listen to the cry that is coming out of creation. Paul's discourse on creation, which he likens to a woman in labor "groaning in travail," tells us something about how to listen to the call of the earth:

> For the creation waits with eager longing for the revealing of the sons of God; for the creation was subjected to futility, not of its own will but by the will of him who subjected it in hope; because the creation itself will be set free from its bondage to decay and obtain the glorious liberty of the children of God. We know that the whole creation has been groaning in travail together until now; and not only the creation, but we ourselves, who have the first fruits of the Spirit, groan inwardly as we wait for adoption as sons, the redemption of our bodies.
>
> (Rom. 8:19–23)

Paul is aware of creation's subjection to futility, its bondage to death and decay, its transitoriness. But he also hears its cry for fulfillment, its longing to transcend the given.

There are basically two different ways to listen and respond to the call of the unfulfilled creation. Some deny creation's cry for liberation. They hear a death rattle resounding throughout creation, not the birth pangs of freedom. They perceive nature as disturbingly indifferent to human hope. Some, like the early Camus, find in nature's indifference a "mournful solace." In the final chapter of *The Stranger*, Camus embraces "the benign indifference of the universe" as the brother of the exiled self.[6] He does not hear creation's cry as an echo of the human hope for freedom; he interprets the groaning of creation as testimony to the isolation of the human being. To the nihilistic Camus, nature is cold.

When Paul listens to the groaning of the universe, he hears something quite different. He interprets creation's cry as the expression of its eager longing for liberty. From the throes of its labor, something new will be born. Creation's groaning is not a death knell but a call to life, a call to hope. We need to understand the call to hope in relation to our participation in creation. It is for us that creation waits, for "the revealing" of the sons and daughters of God. If we were to reveal ourselves as co-creators, as those who participate in creation, we would set free humankind and the rest of creation from bondage to futility and decay. The essence of creation is not death and indifference but life, and life in abundance.

Our participation in creation in the interest of life necessitates good work. Out of good work, a new life, something different from the industrialized society in which we now live, something not death-bound, will emerge. Workers who are able to produce to meet the needs of their communities without doing violence to nature reconcile work and creation. We are all called to this task of reconciliation. In the Catholic tradition, Christ and the saints are often depicted as workers. They are pictured amid their tools, their nets, their sickles, or surrounded by the fruits of their labor, especially food. These images extol the participation of workers in the sanctification of the earth. In the religious culture of the bourgeoisie, however, Christ is typically portrayed as the precious baby in the manger or, in a sentimental way, as the sufferer on the cross. We mainstream Protestants have forgotten about Christ the worker. The concept of workers' participation in Christ's reconciliatory work sounds almost blasphemous to our ears. Yet we fail to see the blasphemy in the denial of a worker's dignity under wage slavery.

If we examine the life and work of Jesus of Nazareth, we find the son of a carpenter working among fishermen and the unemployed, many of them belonging to the poorest of the poor. We discover a Jesus who by caring for and healing the oppressed and the outcast responded to the needs of his society. Jesus and his friends envisaged new forms of community, free from domination, in which nobody would be called "rabbi" or "master." If Jesus' death is seen as the consequence of his work, then the reconciliatory meaning of human work becomes clear. Instead of wasting the best years of our lives meaninglessly in the pursuit of personal wealth, we may join him in understanding that work is the way in which we are personally involved in God's ongoing creation and the redemption of the world.

Through good work, we can further the redeeming transformation of creation, restoring harmony between it and the human community. As the church fathers proclaimed, before the resurrection life was brutal and meaningless; human beings did not participate in creative work but were subjugated to the masters and the power structures, the principalities and powers, of "this world." Once Christ, through his struggle and crucifixion, gained kingship (as the old image would have it), he gave the world back to the control of the working people, the sons and daughters of God. This version of redemption shows clearly how far our contemporary theologizing has moved away from a reconciliatory understanding of both creation and redemption. Mainstream Christianity has reduced the meaning of Christ's salvation to an inward event; it has produced the individual who claims to be saved but who has neither changed nor become an agent of change. This tendency to isolate Christian faith from the social order has meant, among other things, that mainstream theology has failed to address work in the context of creation and redemption. It has ignored the worlds of pain created by the structural organization of our work. It has unconsciously or often even cynically obscured our creation as workers in the image of "the great artist." Christianity has a long record of complicity in bad, meaningless, or harmful work. This is the result not just of insufficient ethical reflection but also of the inability to perceive Christ's work in returning the world to its people. Resurrection from sin's power happens in good work. We still wait for good work. Through good work we are revealed, in our creative empowerment, as the children of God.

NOTES

1. Cf. Dorothee Sölle, *Of War and Love* (Maryknoll, N.Y.: Orbis Books, 1983), pp. 120, 122.

2. Marc H. Ellis, *Peter Maurin: Prophet in the Twentieth Century* (New York and Toronto: Paulist Press, 1981), p. 141.

3. Robert F. Drinan, *Beyond the Nuclear Freeze* (New York: Seabury Press, 1983), p. 8.

4. E. F. Schumacher, *Good Work* (New York: Harper & Row, 1979), p. 79.

5. Ibid., p. 54.

6. Albert Camus, *The Stranger*, trans. Stuart Gilbert (New York: Vintage Books, 1954), p. 154.

10

Sexuality and alienation

God created us as workers and lovers. To be created in God's image means to be able to work and to love. It is with good reason that I attempt to construct a theology of creation out of the fabric of adulthood, the point in the life cycle when human strength, activity, and creational power are at their height. I am skeptical of theologies that focus exclusively on the boundary phenomena of birth and death, thereby making the church into an institution responsive only to the very young and the very old. To talk about our sexuality and our work is to talk about the fundamental activities of our adult lives, in which we experience the intensity of failure and the felicity of success. What happens to us in our work and in our relationships shapes our life with God and is therefore inseparable from our religious life. We live out our co-creatorship in work and love.

If the image of God is eclipsed or distorted through wage labor, so it is also through our sexual arrangements. There is a connection between alienated labor and the fate of sexuality in capitalist society. The exploitative and alienating social context that we have generated in turn shapes and defines who we are. Modern sexual relationships, overwhelmingly characterized by low self-esteem and cynicism, are the extensions of an exploitative society. We have to ask ourselves why our sexual arrangements, our "tightly, coercive predefined modes of feeling and action between women and men," as psychologist Dorothy Dinnerstein describes the human malaise, are so hopeless.[1] How are these arrangements determined by our working conditions? The crux of the matter seems to lie in the repression of human needs resulting from the ascendancy of exchange value in capitalist society. When labor is geared to exchange value and the universal need for money, our human relationships are not immune to the laws of exchange production. It is an illusion to think that people who work from nine to five for exchange value, treating their own work and their relationships to co-workers and products according to the rules of commodity exchange, can then return home and relate to others and to themselves as unalienated human beings capable of fulfilling their suppressed needs. The person who devotes his energies to the corporation at the expense of his personal identity, the one who responds to the organization's demand for loyalty by sacrificing all his time in its service, has determined the fate of his sexuality as well. It is not time, quantitatively speaking, that is at stake, but time's quality: If from nine to five "time is money," how can time after five o'clock be different, be free, be a time for lovers?

The early Marx used the words "estrangement" and "alienation" to characterize human work during the initial stages of industrialization. In his later work, Marx introduced in place of alienation the term "commodity fetishism." Commodity fetishism is a concept Marx developed out of the distinction between use value and exchange value to explain how the idolization of commodities and exchange value not only leaves our desires unfulfilled but even destroys our most human needs. "Need" in Marx's framework is to me interchangeable with what we in religion call "soul": Just as our needs can be manipulated and distorted, the soul can be lost, forgotten, destroyed. What are our authentic needs? I have spoken in this book about the human need for interrelatedness and communion. The wish to be part of a greater unit, the desire to transcend the limitations of the self, is an expression of the "creative-integrative, constructive-reparative human urge" that Freud called "eternal eros."[2] This urge moves us to create larger and larger units, that is, more and more comprehensive human connections and levels of communication. Relationship is central to human life. In the beginning was the relation, as Buber said. All things are fundamentally social, and it is because of the centrality of relatedness that I have rejected a God who is autonomous, remote, and neither desires nor needs the other.

Yet relationship under capitalism is a commodity. Our instincts and passions are largely excluded from social intercourse in capitalist society. We work for exchange value, even though money cannot satisfy real needs, and so the craving for money becomes endless. Analogously, the search for sexual objects is limitless, because the utilitarian or exchange value of bodies does not satisfy actual needs for sex and love. Our need for relationship is repressed, for the true aims of our social needs are substituted by false aims, namely, exchange aims. Because the real aims of our wishes and instincts are not met, we remain unsatisfied. Hence the compulsion to repeat the past is inevitable. The aim of sexuality is deflected from the concrete and unique person to her physical attributes or her aesthetic packaging. The person is turned into an object, a sexual commodity to be possessed or purchased like any other commodity. What is purchased or possessed is abstract sexuality—an abstract "sexy object." Anonymous sex, in which people pursue immediate gratification of their erotic desires with any partner, or the "sport sex" of the well-trained sexual athlete epitomize abstract sexuality; sensation is separated from feeling and expectation, sexuality from human commitment, and loving from knowing.

When a commodity has no use value in itself, at least not for the producer or the buyer, it can become a fetish solely on the basis of its exchange capacity. In theological language, we would call this phenomenon "idolatry," the adoration of things we have made ourselves as godlike. In an exchange society everything that has lost its original useful quality can become grist for commodity fetishism. This applies specifically to sexuality. Any part of the human body (legs, genitals, breasts, buttocks, and the like) can be turned into a sexual fetish for sale. Standardized beauty or sexiness in general or these partial sexual fetishes are attached to other products to enhance their marketability. The illusion is created that what we buy is beauty or sexiness, while the actual use value of the product is obscured. The aim of sexuality is thrust back into unconsciousness, and we are compelled to buy again because we failed to "get" the sexiness for which we yearned.

As our work and our products fall prey to the near universal preoccupation with exchange value—money—our need for sexual communication is repressed. Within this void, a standardization of what is beautiful and sexy grows up, youthfulness being a primary component of the standardized notion of beauty. The movie *Harold and Maude* portrays what happens to people when communion between persons is reduced to physical contact and when beauty is standardized and abstracted from individuality and personhood and turned into a commodity. Harold, the film's young protagonist, is in desperate need of someone who will care about him with integrity. He lives an alienated life in his mother's household where genuine relationships have been forfeited in a dizzying pursuit of money, material goods, social connections, and sex. Harold's mother and two of her prominent companions, a general and a priest, continually offer him attractive young women to uplift his flagging spirits and to "make him into a man." Rejecting their offers and their notion of manhood, Harold, reminiscent of Hamlet, retreats further into himself and feigns madness to ward off their entreaties. He yearns for something beyond the commodity fetishism of his mother's world, where genuine needs are suppressed by subtle terrorism and false needs are propagated and substituted. Love finally comes to Harold in what is viewed as an absurdity by his mother's world: a love affair between him and a very old woman.

The irony underlying *Harold and Maude* is that love is a stranger in a consumeristic world. Appearing in the guise of an old woman with her wrinkles, her frailty, and her readiness for death, genuine love remains invisible. In our consumeristic world, love has become a matter of buying. "I love that vase" expresses exactly what love in the consumer society means: "I want to have it, to buy it." The sense of buying and having has become, as Marx said, the "sense par excellence," the "sense of all senses." Economics has replaced religion as "the ultimate concern," to use Tillich's phrase.

As our needs for meaningful work, self-respect, dignity, and noncompetitive social relations have been overtaken by consumerism, so have the family and our sexual relationships. It is superficial to understand the collapse of traditional values, the crisis of the family, and the celebration of promiscuous sexuality simply as moral issues that a self-declared "moral majority" can redeem. The collapse of traditional values is the consequence of an economy that extols exchange value over use value, profit over people, production over human work, capital over labor. The economic option for exchange value at the expense of use value has thwarted not just the objective aims of production but also our subjective drives, instincts, and needs. This system has changed our relations, stunting our capacity to relate to others. In a class society, we cannot freely relate to members of another social class; in a racist society, whites cannot stretch out their hands to their brothers and sisters of color; and in a sexist society it is dangerous to expect men to show respect for or solidarity with women.

For the most part, advertising is a means of cultural repression that has done more for the destruction of genuine, humanistic values, such as respect for the elderly, willingness to help the poor and the handicapped, and tolerance of group differences, than many other tools of mass education. Anyone who tries to raise children with a set of values different from those of mainstream culture knows that. Most conflicts I have had with my own children (up to about age twelve) centered around their having been indoctrinated through mass media to want and to purchase certain things in an effort to gain peer approval. The immediate purpose of advertising is to sell products, but in advanced capitalist societies advertising has taken on a new role in mass education. Its purpose is not only to sell Brand X but also to create a climate in which selling, buying, bargaining, and saving become the most important human activities. People's worth then hinges on their relationship to money. Advertising reduces the whole of human activity to units of production and the consumption of things. Advertising has become an erotic science, and it uses women in particular as things on a par with any other marketable merchandise. Take, for example, a 1980 advertisement for the investment magazine *American Business*. In the form of a signed letter from a woman whose photograph dominates the page, it reads:

> DARLING: I like men who like money—who know how to get it, enjoy it. I'm betting you're one of them, and I'd like to give you a subscription to a magazine that's SINFULLY enriching. . . . Hurry. Don't keep me waiting. C'mon now, be a darling.[3]

Because human beings are not yet ready for total capitalism, they have to be socialized to it. In the conventional nuclear family, man is the producer and woman is the consumer. The woman therefore becomes the special target and victim of this new type of mass education. She was sold before; now she too becomes the buyer and adapts herself to the cycle of prostitution. Once the mere object, now she is the agent of the transformation of human needs. The overall goal of this new type

of mass education is the molding of human desire. Typical of the pleth-
ora of advertisements aimed at the female consumer, one major retail
store advertisement reads:

> Thank you Don Sayres, for my black velvet nights. Now all I need is one
> silver cloud. These nights, most of my little evenings are spent with Don
> Sayres for Gamut—dining by a window overlooking the world, seeing my
> friend's new show after it opens. And me, the center of it all, in a trouser
> turn-out just special-occasion enough.[4]

The full-length photograph of a woman dressed in a black velvet pant-
suit spans the page. She is wide-eyed and open-mouthed; her expression conveys a mixture of coldness, idiocy, and greed.

"For where your treasure is, there will your heart be also" (Matt.
6:21). Advertising dictates where our treasures ought to be. Its teaching has three educational aims: reduction and denial of our collective
needs, repression of our authentic individual needs, and creation of
artificial needs. In an industrialized society, everyone has needs in common with other people. For example, all need decent jobs, clean water,
public means of transportation, education, and work oriented to peace
instead of the production of death. Yet none of these most crucial needs
shows up in advertisements. Our wishes and values are silenced and reduced to private ones. The language of dream, wish, and hope plays an
important role in our lives, but people in advertisements do not have
needs other than materialistic and individualistic needs. This is particularly dangerous for minorities or underprivileged groups such as
women and the poor. They are taught to forget what they really need;
they become depoliticized; they are dissuaded from even dreaming of a
fully human life. This pernicious state of affairs damages women,
specifically in relation to their sexual needs. Advertising invites women
to trade in the risky, adult search for an adequate partner for the child-
ish hope of getting or buying a spouse just like any other piece of
merchandise.

The individual's need for respect, love, and security cannot simply be
silenced. Therefore advertising must manipulate these needs. Fulfillment is promised by buying this or that product: "Warmth for a
whole life" . . . Buy this brand-name oven. Consumerism is the religion

of a society that perverts any human desire for personal relations into a desire for things. The original wish to be loved is still there, but it is assailed into unconsciousness. Consciously people wish to get, to have, and to buy; the unconscious power of the deeper wish is tapped by advertising to stimulate consumerism. And because what we repress returns again and again, the repressed wish must be cheated each time it surfaces. Advertising encourages us never to be satisfied or content. How could we be, with the vast array of purchasable commodities before us?

Our fundamental human needs are prostituted by the culture of advertisement in its never-ending creation of new, superfluous needs: "You would call them a luxury. I call them a necessity." The basic material needs for food, shelter, and clothing allow for an almost infinite diversity. Therefore, diversity is an important value in the culture of advertisement. The search for the simplified life style that inspired Henry David Thoreau and other representatives of the best American traditions is eschewed by the advertising industry. Simplicity is construed as the emblem of preindustrialized societies or of narrow-minded provincialism. Middle-class women are special victims of advertising's creation of artificial needs, particularly when they grow dissatisfied with the traditional female role. Instead of changing their roles, they are instructed to change the objects they consume.

We may understand the advertising experts as high priests of a new religion. Who is the speaker in the language of the ads? It is the voice of god. Only an omniscient and almighty god may speak as the advertisers do. This god knows our sorrows and concerns: "I understand you. You've worked enough." This god is compassionate and benign: "Forget about the office for three days. Have it your way." This god knows how to fulfill our wishes: "Believe me, you know it's true." Seemingly benign, this god has his demands. The believer is enjoined to obey the commandments of this god immediately: "Buy now." The familiar religious appeal to act "right now" resounds again and again. The relationship to this deity is very personal; it is to this god's special initiate that the voice is directed: "This is reserved for you." His or her dignity is unique and clearly demarcated from other, ordinary, undistinguished people: "The individual man who won't be compromised by the ordinary"; "fresh, natural, named just for you." The conventional religious words like sin, faith, trust, and truth are co-opted for new purposes. Blessing is bestowed from above ("how lucky to have been born a woman"); a total promise accompanies the new coat or the trip to Florida. Salvation is promised and damnation is threatened: You must buy if you would be saved. The punishment of eternal loneliness will be your lot if you do not purge your body of its natural odors. Eternal mockery menaces the man with the worn-out furniture.

There is something terribly wrong with a society that spoils our dreams and catches our souls in the gilded prison of buyable things. Our needs cannot be satisfied by things. We require communication, being together with others; indeed, we need the mutual give-and-take of love. We may say, from a religious perspective, that ultimately only God can still our needs. But I hasten to add that God acts solely through human beings and not through material idols. The God who can still our needs is not an extramundane giver ready to satisfy all our worldly desires miraculously. *Only God can still our needs* is a statement of faith that first and foremost expresses the limitlessness of our needs that no thing, no available or buyable object, can still. Second, it is an affirmation of our dependency: It is not through our individual efforts that we get what we need; we are part of the web of life and we depend on others for our fulfillment. Third, that only God can still our needs means that to be in need is not a lamentable condition of our existence, nor an ephemeral one. Need is intrinsic to human life, and the most fundamental need we know is the need to be needed.

We cannot afford to ignore the present threat to our need to be needed. Love has two enemies today. One is an old patriarch, the other a stylish young man. The old man prefaces everything he has to say with "Thou shalt not." He loves to be in control of all things, especially women. He stands for traditional religious and familial values, speaking out against premarital sex, reproductive rights, and homosexuality. He tries to enforce his will through legal and extralegal regulations. He is repressive and coercive as a father or as the head of a church board. The neurotic conflict he usually engenders is the Oedipal conflict. Because the new enemy of love eschews these forms of coercion, it is more difficult to detect his equally compulsory features. The new enemy assures us that sex is a commodity and not "sin"—a word he would not allow to pass over his lips. He rejects moralism. His repression of our need for relationship works through consumerism. He exploits our feelings but does not oppress them. He trivializes sexual relationships and makes sex into a commodity. The neurotic or pathological conflict he produces is narcissism.

Since the mid-1970s psychiatrists have used the Greek myth of Narcissus to explain the problems of their clientele. In place of Oedipus, Narcissus has surfaced as the new bearer of frustration, neuroticism, and malaise. Narcissus, the son of a river god, was a young man of irresistible beauty. All the females who saw him longed to be his, but he did not even notice them. The most radiant nymph by the name of Echo fell in love with him and was so hurt by his coldness that she pined away until nothing remained of her except her voice, the echo. When the gods learned of her fate, they were enraged and sought to punish Narcissus. Nemesis, the goddess of revenge, was appointed to carry out their plan. She caused Narcissus to fall in love with himself. Bending over a clear pool for a drink, he fell in love with his own reflection and was gripped with a burning desire for himself. He was so unable to leave the handsome youth whom he saw reflected in the water that he remained fixated on his own image until he died. Even as his spirit crossed over the river to the realm of the dead, he leaned out of the boat to catch one last glimpse of himself in the mirroring waters.

Narcissus is beautiful but unable to feel anything. He is unrelated to the world around him. He has no interests that would relate him to others. He is cut off from the needs of other people. For Narcissus, his death means the end of everything. Both past and future are inconsequential; what counts are the moments of self-mirroring, nothing more. His beauty is untouchable and ageless. The Greek myth tells us that the kind nymphs who wanted to bury his body could not find it. Where it had once lain, there was only a lovely new flower, to which they gave his name, Narcissus. Is this not a story about our time? Is this not a story about ourselves? Do we want to be beautiful, ageless, untouchable, and entranced with ourselves? Is this our life's priority?

Let us reflect on the Narcissus myth as it operates today. An advertisement in the *New York Times* for the women's magazine *Cosmopolitan* contained a picture of a good-looking blonde, who seemingly knows what she wants from life, and the following text:

First he said we couldn't marry so soon after his divorce. He had to breathe a little. O.K. He breathed for a year or so. Then he said the children were going through a stage and he wanted to devote more time to them. Then his job got very demanding and he couldn't take time off during my vacation. Are you ready? We're getting married this Sunday. O.K. He has given me a hard time. But when I think about it, his explanations weren't all that unreasonable. At least, that's what my favorite magazine says. They say so much about loving men. I couldn't tell you a thousandth of it. Oh, I love that magazine. I guess you could say I *am* the cosmopolitan girl.[5]

When I read a text like this I have to breathe a little too. The cynicism is so undisguised. A man is an object that you have to procure through careful planning and the right strategy. The modern—meaning self-conscious and critical—woman knows how to do that with the help of her favorite magazine. There is a need for technical, psychological know-how in order to manipulate a man into marriage. The recipes are not given in the advertisement but implied: "They say so much about loving men." The qualities of the object, the man, are not disclosed either. The new consciousness that came out of the women's movement has been manipulated ("his explanations weren't all that unreasonable") in a sellout to narcissistic culture.

Narcissus, as he shows up today in the psychiatrist's office, does not take only the form of a handsome young man. The cosmopolitan girl, as advertised, is equally occupied with mirroring herself, observing herself, and enjoying herself. Even the difficulties of her man, who from her own description seems weary of marriage, are grist for consumerism. The past he is still working through is siphoned off. The future is deadlocked. After listening to her message, one is prompted to ask the young woman, "What next?" The culture of narcissism tells us how to make more out of our lives, which means more traveling, more sumptuous food, more sex, and making and spending more money on items strictly for individual consumption. No future is anticipated or planned for in the society of individuals. Nothing that would transcend individual self-realization has any importance. Both religion and politics seem altogether useless; it sounds like a fairy tale that they were once the true expressions of relations between people, media of communication that united and separated human beings. Communicating, sharing, being able to relate to one another is effectively ruled out. That would involve challenges and struggles different from the ones known about in the culture of narcissism. In most ancient cultures, happiness consisted of transcending, crossing a frontier that was considered hitherto untraversable. But in the culture of narcissism we remain entranced before our waters, incapable of movement.

We are threatened by both the old and the new enemies of love who sometimes form a strange alliance. The repression of the old culture was based on nature and a seemingly natural understanding of human sexuality that made procreation its aim. Enforced procreation is the mode and ideological basis of sexual conservatism, or the old enemy of love. Inside the Christian tradition, heterosexism and misogny are the most blatant forms of hostility against sexuality. The resistance of most churches to sex education, birth control, and procreative rights is an outrageous fact, especially when compared to their minimal resistance to the arms buildup, education for war, aggression, and militarism. Compulsory procreation is buttressed ideologically as an a priori condition of creation or as an indication of normalcy and the natural mode of human life. And on this basis, gay and lesbian relationships are condemned. Christian repression against those who "come out" (because they know how destructive remaining "in the closet" is for the true meaning of human sexuality) is a grievous assault on our being created in God's image. Such repression sustains a culture of domination through manipulation of fear and guilt by religion.

A friend of mine was asked in a job interview, "Is it true that you are homosexual?" His response was, "I did not ask you whether you are heterosexual. If you had asked me whether I steal silverware or seduce small children, I would have understood the question." Clearly the interviewer, a clergyman, was alienated from his own sexuality to the extent that he could implicitly proscribe another's.

The new enemy of love is no less threatening to a theology of sexuality that understands the human being as inherently a being in relation. The culture of consumerism has developed its own mechanism of peddling sex as a commodity. Our sexuality, in the widest sense of the word, concerns our capacity for relationship. When sexuality is reduced to the sexual act or to genital orgasm, the integration of the whole person in a relationship is hindered and the potential extent of ecstasy is diminished. Reductionism is the shrinking of a broader, multidimensional phenomenon into a smaller, well defined, and more controllable one. That which in reality manifests a thousand qualities is reduced to a defined, measurable quantity. When sexuality is confined to the genital act, other sensuous bodily experiences are ignored, the so-called partial drives are forfeited. The result of this reduction of human sexuality to the genital act is an impoverishment of feeling, pleasure without imagination, and an absence of spirit. Experiences of sexuality are not shared, so that sex does not lead to any growth of the self. The dream of anonymous sex is the dream of the marketplace where one object is readily exchangeable for another. This heresy suggests that wholeness is impossible.

One of humanity's oldest hopes, a hope that recurs in visions of fulfilled sexual relationships, is the wish to reconcile the rational and irrational layers of our being. This wish finds expression again and again in great art, especially classical art. I am thinking of the works of Shakespeare, Rembrandt, and Mozart as well as twentieth-century creations by Picasso and Brecht, to name just a few. When, for example, we listen to Mozart's *Magic Flute*, we become aware of art's reconciliatory function and integrative power. We are lured by the promise of art, namely, to free "that wordless alogical being who lives inside each of us."[6] Authentic praise of God is possible only if all that is within us can be released in praise, if no part of the self is excluded or suppressed. But our consumer society, dominated as it is by what the Italian writer and filmmaker Pier Paolo Passolini has called "hedonistic fascism," pushes us to suppress our personalities and to give up on the integration of our diverse forces and potentials. A society ruled by the marketplace cannot accommodate our need to be whole, and so it must disavow the need and defend our surrender of wholeness as an inevitability.

NOTES

1. Dorothy Dinnerstein, *The Mermaid and the Minotaur: Sexual Arrangements and Human Malaise* (New York: Harper & Row, 1976), p. 3.
2. Ibid., p. 10.

3. This advertisement appeared in the *New York Times*, February 21, 1980, p. B9.

4. This advertisement appeared in the *New York Times*, September 7, 1976, p. L7.

5. This advertisement appeared in the *New York Times*, n.d.

6. Dinnerstein, *Mermaid and Minotaur*, p. 11.

11

Ecstasy and trust

Sometimes when I listen to a sexually repressed person or find myself in a group of people who are sexually alienated, I feel an urgent need for a language that transcends analytical discourse. I need a language that goes beyond depicting the deficiencies and failures of our sexual arrangements. It is not enough to explain why a particular psychosexual history makes someone unable to love or to analyze the socioeconomic conditions that make sexual alienation inevitable. The need for self-expression, for sharing not just our defeats and our cynicisms but our hopes and dreams as well, the need to make public what we feel and expect is not satisfied by analytical talk. Other forms of language are required; explanation is not enough. I need a vision that can be shared with others. We need a language that speaks with integrity and renews the promise of happiness.

There are biblical passages, phrases, and words in which I hear a voice different from the one emanating from my world, one that points to the vision we still lack. For example, when I read Gen. 2:25 ("And the man and his wife were both naked and were not ashamed") or 1 John 4:18 ("There is no fear in love, but perfect love casts out fear . . . the [one] who fears is not perfected in love"), I encounter a language of ecstasy that analytical discourse cannot encompass. Both biblical texts presuppose the reality of shame and fear. They speak to my own situation, especially as a woman conditioned to shame and fear. But they also transcend what is.

There is a language that the human family has developed in diverse dialects. That language is religion. Religion is an attempt to talk about wholeness, blessedness, and happiness and to transcend what we already know and can name. Religious language, talking about God, angels, miracles, healing, freeing, resurrecting, is a language that moves us beyond the status quo of our own lives. And that is what happiness does to us. It propels us beyond ourselves. I need religion because I need to express my happiness in a language that surpasses the quotidian world.

Writing about the need for a language that nourishes and challenges our feelings and experiences, I observe that my mind wavers between saying "I" or "we." Is my sense of the power of religious language merely subjective, valid only for myself? Is it only because of my Christian cultural heritage, raised as I was on Bach's oratorios and Rembrandt's paintings, that the language of the Bible speaks to me, consoles me, moves me? What about other people who either do not understand this particular language or who have even been injured by its repressive uses? There are so many broken brothers and sisters who long ago have given up on praising creation and who have not been helped by any religious tradition to discover beauty and joy in their own sexuality.

Even students of theology sometimes distrust churchly language. I remember a classroom discussion when I tried to share with seminarians my emergent vision of love relationships. There it hit me that for many people vision often connotes normative rules or divine commandments. There is a distinction, however, between a commandment and a vision. The Ten Commandments can be understood as the ethical proscriptions of a deity who admonishes us that we "shalt not" commit certain acts. But it is also possible to read the Ten Commandments in a future-oriented sense—"Thou will not" do this or that—almost as a prophecy that has a much more inviting, nonthreatening character. A vision of love and sexual relatedness does not partake of threat or intimidation. With regard to human sexuality, there is no ethics that would enforce specific conduct, because sexual ethics arises out of an agreement between free partners. Even the more subtle forms of coercion or discrimination have no basis in a theological reflection on sexuality. In this sense, good theology is marked by liberality and tolerance.

Yet the absence of oppressiveness alone does not make for a liberating perspective. A radical perspective on sexual liberation is different from a liberal one. A radical perspective goes beyond permissiveness as the sine qua non of freedom by virtue of its effort to interrelate the theme of sexual relationships with actual sexual arrangements in a given historical situation. I have attempted to identify the Western historical context by its accelerating propensity toward consumerism, hedonistic fascism, and sex-as-commodity. A vision can arise only from a concrete context; otherwise it remains an illusion and the repository of romanticism in its most tarnished form. If liberalism lacks a vision, liberation theology offers a different perspective, a vision of love in light of the historical project of our createdness. Our creation in God's image means that we are created to become lovers like God. This is part of the ontological project that we work out in our historical project.

The historical project of human sexuality today differs from that of other historical periods. The horizon of our understanding is the paradigm shift from nature to history. This shift is objectively necessitated by the overpopulation of the earth. Because nature has linked human sexuality to procreation, pleasure and procreation have been interconnected in human history. Moreover, this natural linkage has long been used as leverage for oppressing women in particular. The biblical narrative on creation, however, offers a different, liberating perspective on human sexuality, as biblical scholar Phyllis Trible has shown. Using the methodology of rhetorical criticism to investigate the biblical creation myth, Trible demonstrates that sexual differentiation corresponds to the image of God and that it "does not mean hierarchy but equality."[1] Both male and female in the Genesis account receive the divine blessing; both are addressed by God; both are given dominion over the earth; both are granted equal power.[2] There is sexuality and sexual difference, but there is no domination of the male over the female. And according to this tradition, sexuality and sexual pleasure are not necessarily or "naturally" linked to procreation. As Trible observes, in the Genesis account procreation is shared by all biological organisms, but sexuality is specific to humankind. Only the human being is designated by God as male and female (Gen. 1:27), and this designation, Trible maintains, "pertains not to procreation but to the image of God."[3] It is precisely with this connection between our sexuality and our creation in God's image that the historical project of redefining our sexuality must begin.

The linkage between sexual pleasure and procreation provided the basis for two forms of dualism in Western history: the spiritualistic dualism of spirit and body and the sexist dualism of male and female. Both dualistic traditions fostered the hostility against sex that became characteristic of Western mainstream culture. Today the hostility against both women and sexuality presents itself in the three interlocking modes of heterosexism, rejection of procreative choice, which is most visible in the crusade against abortion, and idolization of the nuclear family, falsely identified as *the* family. Sexual conservatives still operate according to the paradigm of naturalism to uphold the link between sexuality and procreation. When procreation is considered "normal" and "natural," heterosexuality becomes a fetish. It has to be enforced, and other forms of sexuality must be repressed. I remember a church conference on homosexuality in which a man, a doctor at a public health clinic, jumped up and shouted angrily: "I am not homosexual! I am not heterosexual! I'm just sexual!" His pronouncement unleashed a liberating laughter throughout the church. The astonishing ease with which people categorize and label one another was checked. Heterosexism as mandatory heterosexuality was unmasked. At least some of the people in attendance made the shift from nature to history.

Conservative Christians have not yet moved from a naturalistic understanding of human sexuality to a historical, hence biblical, understanding of it. They deny, often unconsciously, the historical project of our being created for freedom. They misread God's invitation to participate in the reality of creation as a call to a sort of biologism, as if there were no other way to participate in creation besides procreation. There is a kernel of truth in a sexually conservative position insofar as it stresses the self-transcendent quality of human sexuality. Our bodies are not simply pleasure machines, and love is two people looking not only at each other but also at a third cause, to paraphrase Saint-Exupéry. In fulfilled sexual relationships, partners yearn to go further, to explore each other and the world more fully. Love's self-transcendent quality has its biological basis in procreation. The wish to have a child together is one of the most elementary expressions of love, and its absence in one partner may signal a serious lack of commitment to the relationship. But giving birth to offspring is only one among many possible expres-

sions of love's self-transcendent quality. The significance of our sexuality is aptly stated by James Nelson:

> Sexuality is a sign, a symbol, and a means of our call to communication and
> communion. . . . The mystery of our sexuality is the mystery of our need to
> reach out to embrace others both physically and spiritually. Sexuality thus
> expresses God's intention that we find our authentic humanness in rela-
> tionship.[4]

In any long-term relationship there is a need for a common "project,"
something the lovers want to accomplish in their world, such as building a house, tilling a garden, doing social work in an impoverished
neighborhood, running a business, or, to name the most traditional but
by no means universal project last, raising a family. This is true for all
intimate relationships. I remember a childhood friendship in which a
boy and I, both age eight, devoted all our time, imagination, and energy to building a tree house. It was our dream, our secret, our project.
A common project is essential in a love relationship. And if the project
is too small, constraining the growth of its creators, the relationship
may break down. The greatest project I can name is the quest for justice, what Jesus called building the kingdom of God. Hunger for justice
is part of the love energy that is set free in sexual relationships.

My aim here is to develop a religious vision of love and sexual-relatedness. How might we identify fulfilled relationships in which we
would realize our being created in the image of love? I will examine
four dimensions of love: ecstasy, trust, wholeness, and solidarity. God
created us as beings with a sexual identity so that we might participate
in the ecstasy of life: "So God created human beings in God's own
image . . . male and female God created them" (Gen. 1:27). There is
a capacity for happiness in the human being that is self-transcending,
causing us to shed our former selves. The sexual experience is a way of
participating in this self-transcendent, creative power.

From a Freudian perspective we may identify love's ecstasy in relation to our psychosexual history. As infants we receive nearly perfect bodily and emotional care, usually from our mothers. Dorothy
Dinnerstein has observed that the world of infancy breeds in us the illusion of the permanent availability of a pleasure-giver and hence the illu-

sion of our own omnipotence. But this illusion is soon crushed; the child discovers that he or she does not own and control the mother's body.[5] The loss of this primal illusion is, at least to some degree, irreparable. It is, as Freud emphasized, a basic human grief with which we have to live. But there are domains in which the infant sense of delight and absolute fulfillment can be reexperienced, for example, in our lovemaking, which is, as Dinnerstein puts it, a "direct attempt to repair the old loss."[6]

To equate the old loss with infancy's feeling of "omnipotence," however, may be an all too patriarchal, Freudian expression for what might instead be called the loss of unity with the all-providing mother. Perhaps "omnirelatedness" more accurately characterizes what we have come from and what we long for. Relatedness to all that lives would then be our original experience, which we lose in the process of differentiating and creating ourselves as individuals. Lovemaking is an attempt to find our way back to the old unity, albeit without renouncing adult levels of knowing and being. Sexual ecstasy reignites in us the "oceanic feeling" of an indissoluble oneness with the surrounding world.[7] Sexual ecstasy affords us "direct recapture of the earliest mode, the unqualified animal-poetic mode of erotic intercourse with the surround."[8] Through the momentary recapture of infancy's euphoric connection to the world, we undo the loss, assuage our grief, and rediscover a kind of passionate, primitive joy in our existence. We overcome the separation we sensed when we were driven out of our mother's womb, when we were expelled from the Garden of Eden. The time of separation and coldness ends; we enter another time. God is with us; we shall not want.

Our capacity for ecstasy is equivalent to our need. The ecstasy of lovemaking frees us to understand our want: how alone, how incomplete, how broken we are without participation in ecstasy. Sexuality is one of the characteristics of life on earth; whatever we may know of other planets, they appear to have no sexual life. The earth is a sexual planet, and we affirm its being good in celebrating the true richness of the human being in loving and in making love. We are erotically connected with the world.

The experience of receiving ecstasy is also the experience of being able to give ecstasy to another person, whom we then free from the loneliness that "is not good" (Gen. 2:18). There is delight in the other-ness and the sameness of the human being when Adam discovers Eve: "This at last is bone of my bones and flesh of my flesh" (Gen. 2:23). It is at this point that the earth creature takes on a new identity, a sexual one. Phyllis Trible interprets "bone of my bones and flesh of my flesh" to mean "unity, solidarity, mutuality, and equality."[9] Adam and Eve are depicted as interdependent beings, and the delight that is expressed in the words "at last" is part and parcel of mutual ecstasy.

We can reach orgasm all by ourselves, but ecstasy depends on mutu-ality. There is a new quest for the meaning of human sexuality that tran-scends the polarities of repression and permission. The values of this new historicized understanding are mutuality, communion, and vulner-ability—all values strictly opposed to both the naturalistic view of sex and the commercial version of sex as commodity. There is a move and a hope to break the *modus vivendi* of our inherited sexual arrangements. Both mutuality in our sexual arrangements and the sharing of our most intimate feelings are impossible without the vulnerability that is cele-brated and embraced as a value by many feminist groups. To keep our-selves vulnerable and to make ourselves even more vulnerable requires a vigilant effort in a commodity society that mutilates our drives and wishes. Whatever destroys mutuality kills ecstasy as well.

Rape is the most hideous denial of our being created in the image of mutual love. And by "rape," I refer not just to the crime but also to the mentality that mythologizes the rapist as the manliest of men and women as seductresses secretly desiring sexual violation. The male sex-ual fantasies portrayed in the novels and films of pre-Fascist and Fascist Germany, for example, reveal the humiliating and misogynist imagina-tion that would be unleashed in World War II, when Jewish, Russian, and Polish women, in particular, became fair game for SS officers and concentration-camp guards.[10] Lack of mutuality, as well as the rapist mentality, is found in many forms. Asked by the judge presiding at a di-vorce hearing when the couple last had intercourse, a woman replied, "He last had intercourse with me three weeks ago. I last had intercourse with him two years ago."

Ecstasy is based on mutuality, which requires our vulnerability. The biblical narrative expresses this in the words: "And the man and his wife were both naked, and were not ashamed" (Gen. 2:25). They did not need to conceal or to minimize their togetherness. They were not ashamed to know each other and themselves. To become conscious means to strip off our clothes and disguises, to become aware of ourselves apart from the social status that is signified by our clothing. When we are naked, we are also defenseless. We have taken off what protects us from wind and cold, as well as what protects us from society and its merciless discoveries of our bulging, aging, or scarred flesh. Many women, unable to extricate themselves from sexual commodity fetishism, are terrified at the prospect of being ridiculed or despised merely for having breasts that are too large or too small or sagging thighs. To be naked means to be without protection; it is to be unarmed. It requires our surrendering the "weapons" that we usually carry around with us. My credit cards, my doctorate, the books I have written—the whole fortress in which I live—are all "clothes" that I have to get rid of in order to love. When we make love we are defenseless and vulnerable. We make ourselves vulnerable, and there is no way to avoid the risk that vulnerability entails.

Human sexuality envisioned as love also involves trust. We are capable of and in want of ecstasy. The same is true for trust and reliability. "Sleeping together" has the double sense of making love to each other and resting together. Beside our progressive drives and wishes, we harbor regressive needs. Sometimes we need to hide, to be small, to be allowed to show weakness and to bear the weakness of another. Trust means that we do not have to fall into despair in times of impotence and frigidity. We need consolation. The experience of being weak without being dominated and abused comes with relationships that are free of fear and subjugation. I can be free of fear only if I am allowed to be weak. "There is no fear in love, but perfect love casts out fear" (1 John 4:18). Learning to love means becoming less and less afraid. This trust dimension of love also rests on the acceptance of our own sexuality. We learn to be fearless in the face of our own sexual expressions. We accept our createdness as sexual beings and learn to celebrate who we are.

The trust dimension is related to our being aware of our own sexuality and that of the other person. One of the few essential commandments of a new sexual ethics is consciousness: We are to know what we do. We should learn to know ourselves, our wishes, and our fears and to express them as clearly as possible. We should not do anything half-consciously or only for the sake of another person. It is necessary to mention that trust as an essential dimension of human loving also means the sharing of responsibilities for preventing unwanted life. In a relationship where the issue of contraception is evaded or pushed off on the woman, there is surely a disastrous lack of trust.

Trust and ecstasy coexist in creative tension. If one fails, the other will sooner or later crumble as well. Gross imbalance between trust and ecstasy upsets the equilibrium of happiness. Many marriages could be described as trust without ecstasy. The ecstatic elements are used up, forgotten, not renewed; because the capacity to bodily console each other is moribund, trust becomes a tensionless triviality, the "habit of loving," as novelist Doris Lessing has called it. The traditional bourgeois marriage with its double standard for men and women has usually meant that ecstasy occurs, if at all, outside the marital relationship, and therefore trust is doomed to dissolution. In the world of sexual consumerism, ecstasy is subsumed under the performance principle of quantifiable orgasms, and the trust dimension is underdeveloped or never learned. The exchange of sexual partners is inevitable. The pursuit of momentary euphoria replaces relationships that grow in length of time and depth of emotion.

Trust in each other enlarges our capacity to reverse roles—to console, to teach, to support each other, to laugh, to weep, and to pray together. All this happens in genuine mutuality, unlike sexual arrangements where the exploitation of the subordinate position of one partner follows the daily pattern of working for exchange value. In a long-term relationship, we move between the poles of ecstasy and trust, sometimes closer to one, sometimes closer to the other, but nevertheless mindful of the polarity. These essential dimensions of our lovemaking are also expressions of our love for God, our relatedness to the source of life. We relate to God in ecstasy and trust, and again, if one of these dimensions withers the other sooner or later follows suit.

In orthodox Christianity there is a dangerous inclination to abandon the ecstatic dimension of our relatedness to God and to embrace trust as the one and only dimension. By contrast, the great saints kept the fire of ecstasy alive and understood our capacity to praise God in creation as a form of participation in life's ecstasy. Organized religion, especially among white northerners, has often extinguished all sparks of ecstasy from its forms of worship. As a white person coming from a rationalistic religious tradition, attending worship in the black community has taught me more about my own religious needs than white forms of religious ritual ever could. I have sensed more ecstasy and more trust in God in black churches. I remember emerging from a church in Harlem with a small group of white friends singing, "See the fire burning in my heart. . . ." We couldn't stop singing.

A nonreligious reader may ask why I try to relate the celebration of our sexuality in mutual ecstasy and trust to religion. Is there a need for God-talk in the midst of love-talk? Is the sexual discourse self-sufficient? What does God-talk add to the experience of human sexuality? Is our trust less conditional if we trust in God? Is our ecstasy stronger if we relate it to the source of all ecstasy? Does it make a difference if we call our sexual give-and-take a sacrament?

Looking for a response to these questions, I found myself returning to Alice Walker's *The Color Purple*, particularly the passage where Shug explains her religious journey to Celie, moving beyond God as the old white man, first to trees, then to the air, to the birds, and on to other people.[11]

> But one day when I was sitting quiet and feeling like a motherless child, which I was, it come to me: that feeling of being part of everything, not separate at all. I knew that if I cut a tree, my arm would bleed. And I laughed and I cried and I run all around the house. I knew just what it was. In fact, when it happen, you can't miss it. It sort of like you know what, she say, grinning and rubbing high up on my thigh.
>
> *Shug*! I say.
>
> Oh, she say. God love all them feelings. That's some of the best stuff God did. And when you know God loves 'em you enjoys 'em a lot more. You can just relax, go with everything that's going, and praise God by liking what you like.
>
> God don't think it dirty? I ast.
>
> Naw, she say. God made it.[12]

This is a mystical text on sexuality and religion. To understand that "God made it"—all our sexual feelings, our ecstasies, and our trust—is to accept ourselves as sexual beings. Our suspicion that sexuality is dirty or trivial then recedes. We surrender our defenses and let go. The conversation between Celie and Shug gets at the core of the religious experience by way of the sexual experience. Both religion and sexuality heal the split between ourselves and the universe. We discover that we are indeed "part of everything" and one with the mystery of life. To talk about God in relation to our sexuality means to be aware of love moving in us, for "in God we live and move and have our being" (Acts 17:28). The expression to be "in" God means that we experience ourselves as both active and passive: We live but are carried forth by life; we move forward but are drawn back into the web of life; we are created and creating.

NOTES

1. Phyllis Trible, *God and the Rhetoric of Sexuality* (Philadelphia: Fortress Press, 1978), pp. 17–18.

2. Ibid., pp. 18–19.

3. Ibid., p. 15.

4. James B. Nelson, *Embodiment: An Approach to Sexuality and Christian Theology* (Minneapolis, Minn.: Augsburg Publishing House, 1978), p. 18.

5. Dorothy Dinnerstein, *The Mermaid and the Minotaur: Sexual Arrangements and Human Malaise* (New York: Harper & Row, 1976), p. 60.

6. Ibid., p. 61.

7. Sigmund Freud refers to the "oceanic feeling" in his *Civilization and Its Discontents* (London: Hogarth Press and the Institute of Psychoanalysis, 1951), pp. 8–9 and passim.

8. Dinnerstein, *Mermaid and Minotaur*, p. 145.

9. Trible, *God and the Rhetoric of Sexuality*, p. 99.

10. See Klaus Theweleit, *Mannerphantasien Frauer, Fluten, Körper, Geschichte* (Hamburg: Rowohlt, 1980).

11. Alice Walker, *The Color Purple* (New York and London: Harcourt Brace Jovanovich, 1982), p. 167.

12. Ibid.

12

Wholeness and solidarity

The conservative, liberal, and radical stances that we identify in economic theory have their counterparts in the politics of sexuality. Sexual conservatives have failed to redeem the sexual needs of people, especially of women, through their tenacious allegiance to biologically determined, gender-specific sex roles. The conservative attempt to safeguard the natural linkage between pleasure and procreation can be sustained only through massive social repression. But repression does not change anything; it only increases the burden of its victims. Conservative efforts to thwart public education about sex and birth control, for instance, do not decrease the number of abortions, but they do jeopardize women's lives. Public discrimination against homosexuals, designed to repress homoeroticism, only serves to further the rapid exchange of partners among gay men, to deplete their opportunities for wholistic relationships. There is a certain helplessness in the conservative position on sexuality.

In recent decades, liberalism's less repressive and more affirmative response to sexuality (in the form of greater acceptance of premarital and extramarital sex, divorce, homosexuality, and abortion) has increased social tolerance toward sexuality. Though by no means fully realized, greater freedom of self-expression in matters of sex is one of liberalism's genuine achievements. Liberalism espouses equality and mutuality as fundamental ethical values in our sexual relationships, but its sexual ethic is flawed because liberalism construes sexuality narrowly as a private contract between two consenting individuals. Hence, liberals have tended to champion sexual freedom without sufficient regard for the

141

socioeconomic dimensions of sexual politics. The isolation of sexual freedom from our need for economic and political freedom betrays the more far-reaching hope for social equality, for transforming life in its entirety.

The best exponents of the New Left student movement in the 1960s called for a social revolution as well as a sexual revolution, epitomized by the slogan "Make love not war." They rediscovered thinkers like Wilhelm Reich, who dreamt of a "Sex-Pol" movement that tied "orgastic potency," or the capacity to surrender oneself in the sexual act, to authentic political freedom.[1] Although the sexual revolution of the 1960s did alter the mores of the United States and consequently of most Western societies, the widespread hope for a new social order did not materialize. Freedom did not lead to more freedom. On the one hand, many men and women who saw themselves as sexually liberated failed to translate their partial liberation from fear and guilt feelings into overturning the structures of injustice that make love impossible. There was liberation from inhibitions, but not liberation into a more just and free world.

On the other hand, the revolutionary edge of sexual protest was blunted by the market's absorption and manipulation of new sexual mores for profit. The perversion of the original aims of the sexual liberation movement was evident in the rise of popular sex manuals that reduced human sexuality to genital conquest. Writing in 1963, one proponent of sexual liberation admonished men to adopt the following philosophy to ensure success in seducing women:

> You are not here primarily to achieve something wonderful during your lifetime, to be of great service to others, to change the course of the world, or to do anything else but (in one way or another that you find particularly appealing) to enjoy yourself.[2]

What I have called the self-transcendent element in human sexuality is forsaken in this passage. Sex is a "nothing but" affair, and there is only one moral imperative attached to it: to enjoy oneself. The thoroughgoing cynicism behind this advice is indispensable to the commercialization of sex, which cannot proceed unless sex first appears trivial, equivalent to any purchasable, exchangeable item. The liberal vision of sexuality as a private matter has been as helpless before this kind of cynicism and commercialization of human sexuality as conservatism has been up against the breakdown of sexual ethics considered normative for generations.

Sexual radicalism differs from both conservative and liberal stances. It goes beyond the dichotomy of threat and tolerance to envision sexual interrelatedness in community. Mutuality from a radical perspective is more than a matter of adult, mutual consent to certain sexual practices. Mutuality is rather the means by which we will break the hold of present gender arrangements necessary to a society that requires repression of sexuality to maintain a system of white, male, heterosexual privilege. A radical perspective on sexuality acknowledges the futility both of conservatism's attempts to restore traditional sexual arrangements and of liberalism's insistence that sexuality is merely a private affair. A radical position recognizes the necessity of connecting the sexual experience with other parts of our lives and integrating the body-self, the community, and the cosmos into a vision of love.

The two essential components of sexuality presented in the previous chapter are not sufficient by themselves. It is necessary to move beyond an exclusively I-Thou framework to encompass two other dimensions of love that fulfill our search for meaning and communion: wholeness and solidarity. Together, ecstasy and trust, and wholeness and solidarity, represent four interconnected dimensions of love, none of which can stand alone or swallow up the other without jeopardizing our potential for mutuality and self-transcendence.

We cannot understand human sexuality apart from the lifelong challenge to become fully human. Conversely, our quest for meaning and communion with others is grounded in our physiological drives and neediness. The interrelatedness of drives, needs, and quest for fulfillment can be expressed from a religious perspective through the concept of sacramentality. Sexuality is a sacrament, a sign of grace in bodily element. According to traditional teaching, the sacrament occurs when the word comes to the element. Take, for example, the element of bread that is shared at the communion service. Bread, the fruit of human labor, is a sign of God's grace. But its sacramental character appears only in conjunction with the interpretive and meaning-giving word. When the celebrant of the communion service repeats Christ's words "This is my body broken for you," word and element come together and the

THE FOUR DIMENSIONS OF SEXUALITY

Wholeness

To Love Is to Be Whole
Multidimensionality
Integration of our physical potencies
   psychical
   intellectual
   aesthetical
   emotional
   spiritual

Trust	*Ecstasy*
To Love Is to Be at Home	To Love Is to Lose Oneself
Consolation	Delight in being alive
Reliability	Mutuality
Regressive drives	Progressive drives
Vulnerability	Self-transcendence

Solidarity

To Love Is to Know
 The inseparability of love and justice
 The inseparability of the private and the public
 Relatedness to others
 Political dimension of eros/agape

symbolic presence of the body of Christ is revealed. Analogously, human sexuality may be understood as a sacramental reality in which the word of love comes to the element of the flesh and interprets its meaning. The sexual act, then, becomes a sign of God's grace.

Christianity has nevertheless contributed much to the prevailing confusion about the meaning of the word "love" and to the distortion of human sexuality. The ancient Greeks did not speak of love in general.

Instead they identified love by its different forms. *Epithymia* referred to the biological urge for sexual release; *eros* signified an intense desire for the beloved; and *philia* corresponded to mutuality and friendship. When the original Christian congregation sought a term to express their relatedness to one another, a form of community that differed in many ways from the surrounding pagan culture, they chose a word rarely used in classical Greek: *agape*. Agape became the primary Christian term for love. According to 1 John 4:8, God is agape, the altruistic, freely offered, nonpossessive power of love. These Greek distinctions are useful if we understand them as four mutually complementary dimensions of love. However, the majority of my theology teachers, whether orthodox, neo-orthodox, or liberal, drew a sharp distinction between the "merely" human love, eros, and the divine love, agape. In *Eros and Agape* (1930), Anders Nygren identified the divine love agape as absolutely different from sexual passion, which by nature is possessive and egocentric. According to Nygren, God's agape is spontaneous, wholly unmotivated by human beings who have no value apart from what God imparts to them. Divine love creates the value of the beloved objects, who in and of themselves have no worth. Consistent with neo-orthodoxy's insistence on God's wholly otherness, Nygren's strict separation of eros and agape operates to devalue sexual love and to widen the distance between the divine and human capacities for loving.

Instead of humanizing eros, the Christian tradition has often brutalized our drives by separating eros and agape, a separation that threatens to erode the source of our vitality.

Instead of working for the integration of love's diverse manifestations, Christianity has supported the compartmentalization and hierarchical ordering of love's power. By deprecating carnal desire, instead of understanding it as a channel through which we come to know ourselves and God, Christianity has betrayed our need for the unconditional. Instead of celebrating our sexuality as a sign of God in our midst, the repressive Christian tradition has destroyed its sacramental character as a sign of grace in bodily form.

Hostility against and repression of sexuality endanger not only our ability to affirm our bodies and celebrate our existence as sexual creatures. Perhaps the worst part of our repressive heritage is that it kills the human impulse toward psychic and communal wholeness by placing the integration of sexuality and love beyond our reach. The celebration of Christian love and the simultaneous condemnation of its most elementary and compelling expression is a contradiction. It is love that impels us to wholeness; love frees us, challenges us, and develops our capacities and potentials.

An intimate relationship that cannot incorporate fundamental aspects of our lives, whether the intellectual, the aesthetical, or the political, dwarfs our ability to give fully to another person. I remember a brief love affair in which I was always anxious that my partner would open his mouth at the wrong moment and say something incredibly trivial. At first I blamed myself for being so mistrusting, but eventually I realized that I could not truncate my intellectual and emotional level of development to accommodate this person. Realizing that I could not allow myself to forget who I was, I ended the relationship. Multidimensionality is necessary in love; in its drive toward wholeness, love rejects partiality. Love's drive toward wholeness even encompasses time. Love integrates the past, present, and future. Lovers need to talk about their pasts, to delve into their childhoods, and to reconstitute their separate histories in relation to each other. As they pursue the past, they also conjure up a future. A love relation that extinguishes what was and will be, both memory and dream, fragments our being in time and reduces love to an escapist moment.

Wholeness is integral to the development of ecstasy and trust. To some readers this statement may seem overly idealistic, a romantic fantasy that can never materialize because there is no single human being capable of fulfilling all our needs. While it is true that one person cannot meet all our needs, we have to distinguish between a relationship that meets all our needs and one that strives to integrate as many aspects of our lives as possible. Wholeness in a relationship does not mean that I do not need anyone or anything else besides you. Such a relationship would be one of absolute dependency. Wholeness in a relationship means the capacity for sharing our needs and fostering our identities. There is no integrity in a relationship that cannot integrate who we are. If it is true that "perfect love" drives out fear, shame, and mistrust, then we should not settle for less.

Casual sexual relationships of the sort we call in German "throwaway relationships" (*Wegwerfbeziehungen*) violate our need for wholeness and destroy our integrity. Even if you have not yet experienced wholeness in a sexual relationship, you should not silence the need for it in your soul. The mutual agreement to constrain ourselves in a one-dimensional relationship distorts our needs. Even if the object of our pleasure fully consents and no one is hurt, as the contemporary rationale goes, our desires for wholeness, mutuality, and self-transcendence are persistently frustrated. When we reduce each other to mere instruments, the sacramental character of lovemaking eludes our grasp. A vision of wholeness in love differs from an illusion or romantic fantasy by virtue of its relatedness to our needs. The desire to be whole cannot be denied except at peril to ourselves. If we attempt to repress this desire, a strange stagnation surfaces. When the depths of ourselves go untapped, our sexual life becomes perfunctory and we dry up.

Opposing our repressive religious heritage is a liberation tradition that teaches us to believe in wholeness, even at times when we are acutely aware of our brokenness and despair. Certain that "God is greater than our hearts" (1 John 3:20), we know that our vision of love is larger than the small part of it we have realized thus far. The Jewish and Christian traditions assume an interconnection between loving and knowing that honors our need for wholeness. In the Hebrew Bible the verb "to know" has two different meanings; one refers to perceiving and understanding, the other to sexual intercourse. In Gen. 4:1, we find the words "Now Adam knew Eve his wife, and she conceived and bore Cain." Now considered archaic, this use of the verb "to know" reveals a forgotten ingredient in love, namely, its cognitive power. If we apply the cognitive connotations of the verb "to know" to our sexuality, then to know someone sexually means being aware of the other, observing and recognizing who he or she is, and experiencing the many facets of the beloved's personality. Love itself has cognitive power. One form of abstract sexuality is to sunder knowing from loving.

Augustine said that we know only what we love. Without eros, there is no genuine *logos*. For the person who strives for wholeness, the erotic impulse is a cognitive one as well. Sex is one way we come to know our partners, ourselves, the community, and the cosmos in which we live. The mind does not grow apart from desire and bodily performance. Sexuality and intellectual curiosity go hand in hand. We impoverish our carnal and emotional desires if we sever them from the desire to know another person deeply, and our knowledge diminishes if it becomes passionless and unrelated to social realities in purpose or result. To know more is to love more, and to love more is to know more. The aim of knowledge is communion, not possession. Authentic knowledge, be it of another person, oneself, or God, is never amenable to possession, control, and domination; it is rather a vehicle for sharing who we are. To know and to make oneself known is a single act in a love that is mutual.

Earlier I stated that some readers may object to my vision of wholistic sexual relationships as hopelessly idealistic. Actually the assumption that asking for wholeness in sexual relationships is asking for too much is widespread. Disillusionment and sexual hopelessness pervade Western societies today. Again and again I hear adults of all ages say that a wholistic approach to sexuality, with its lofty demands, inflates our expectations and is therefore bound to fail. Better that we settle for physical gratification that need not necessarily be tied to personal growth, religious feelings of cosmic relatedness, or the struggle against social injustice. It saddens me when I hear men and women voice this opinion, because I sense in them a tolerance toward self-destruction, an assent to the muting of authentic desire, an embrace of mediocrity, and a willingness to surrender their integrity.

But it troubles me more when I hear women doom a wholistic approach to sexuality, because my hope lies with women, more than with men, to remedy present patterns of injustice owing to our objective socioeconomic disadvantage. I agree with Walther Benjamin, one of the leading philosophers of the Frankfurt school, who said, "Only for the sake of the hopeless hope is given to us."[3] I am afraid that women, because of the objective hopelessness of our situation, may give up on the hope that we, and perhaps we alone, carry within us. I am afraid that women, in the attempt to overcome the inequality of sexual privilege, the double standard in which women are "less free than men to seek 'selfish' sexual pleasure,"[4] may simply adopt rather than transform patriarchal sexual mores. Historically it has been men's prerogative to split off affection from lust and to dissociate the physical from the emotional and spiritual possibilities in love. It has been men's privilege to refrain from treating sex as a serious matter, to reduce the act of loving to a superficiality, and to control and coerce women. But do we women want to imitate the mind-body split, the emotional deprivation, and the crippling of human pride that underlie the system of male privilege?

I am still not ready to abandon wholeness. I assume (with Dinnerstein and others) that women in Western culture have been socialized throughout history to grow up sexually muted, so that the majority never lay claim to their own erotic spontaneity. But within women's inherited disadvantage also lies a unique opportunity. Because of our socialization, women, unlike most men, are forced to work intensely on integrating their emotions into their relationships. The lack of wholeness in a relationship seems to injure us, to affect us more deeply, which means that we continue to be pulled by the promise of wholeness. There is a small voice calling us to an ecstasy that does not occur without wholeness.

I recall an encounter with a renowned European intellectual when I was fourteen years old. Everyone had always spoken to me of this man in reverent tones, but when I met him I was quickly disillusioned by his showy behavior in front of his companion, a pretty blonde of nineteen considered shallow and frivolous by my circle of friends. I remember my shock when I realized the nature of their relationship. Later I confronted my mother with my discovery. She responded that such purely sexual liaisons occurred often and were normal. I was disgusted. I felt that this famous man was taking advantage of a young girl and that both were violating something for which I had no name, something that today I would call love's wholeness.

In my search for sources that illuminate wholeness within the Christian tradition, I find myself drawn to the biblical Song of Solomon. It celebrates sexual love between a young man and woman, the yearning, the ecstasy, the loss and recovery of love. It affirms that "love is strong as death" (Song of Sol. 8:6) and that, like death, love strikes us in our whole being. And it is liberating to see that there is no assumption of fixed gender roles in these poems, for the young woman often takes the initiative. In an assertive, self-aware, inviting voice, she proclaims:

> For love is strong as death,
>   jealousy is cruel as the grave.
> Its flashes are flashes of fire,
>   a most vehement flame.
> Many waters cannot quench love,
>   neither can floods drown it.
>   (Song of Sol. 8:6b–7a)

The Song of Solomon does not mention marriage or any other social institution. It does not focus on procreation or the family. It praises the fulfillment of creation in human sexuality.

As in the Garden of Eden, there are fountains and streams to drink from in Solomon's garden of love. But the difference is that the lovers may invite each other to eat the "choicest fruits" of every tree (4:16c). There is no prohibition attached to their life in the garden, no question of obedience and disobedience. The Song of Solomon stands in clear contrast to the curse tradition of pain, fruitlessness, and dominion found in Gen. 2:4b—3:24. In this series of love poems, work and sexual play in the garden are intertwined:

> My beloved has gone down to his garden,
>   to the bed of spices,
> to pasture his flock in the gardens,
>   and to gather lilies.
> I am my beloved's and my beloved is mine;
>   he pastures his flock among the lilies.
>   (Song of Sol. 6:2–3)

In the Song of Solomon, nature, animals, men, and women partake of the joy, the abundance, the fullness of life in the garden.

There is yet another dimension of a fulfilled relationship that expresses our connection to all that lives. For a long time I wavered about how to name this fourth dimension. Words like "oneness" and "relatedness" came to mind. So did the biblical metaphor "the holy city," for I believe that our reflection on human sexuality is incomplete without a vision of the *polis*. I finally decided to call this sociopolitical dimension of our sexuality "solidarity," the name that the workers' movement of the world has bestowed on what the Christian tradition has called love. To use the word "solidarity" in the 1980s is to evoke images of the Polish workers' union of the same name. This is intentional on my part, for I want to remind us of one of the greatest struggles for freedom in our time.

Genuine erotic love opens the hearts and minds of lovers to other people. This statement may sound banal, but I am afraid that the Christian adherence to a sharp distinction between eros and agape has succeeded in blinding us to this reality of love. To love more is to know more not only of our partner but also of the human community. There is no eros without agape and, I would hasten to add, no agape without eros. Only a superficial perspective would limit relatedness to the exchange between sexual partners.

The trivial myth of the idyllic island where you and I find refuge from a hostile world represents a dangerous form of sexual escapism that betrays our greater need to be united with the world in which we live. Yet this is one of our most enduring and influential cultural myths, celebrated in film, advertising, and other mass media. The myth speaks to us because all of us are sometimes precisely in need of a remote and shining hideaway. And however diverse our dreams about island life may be, they have one thing in common: They are motivated by the suspicion that our real life is elsewhere, not here but far away.

The mass media version of this myth is all the more insidious because it idolizes a specific couple: It is the young, white, heterosexual, healthy, and sleek twosome who occupy the island retreat. They are portrayed as free spirits, unhampered by work, family, and other human relationships and obligations. The media conveys their freedom from worldly concerns in images of vast empty beaches, luxury yachts, birds in flight, and other emblems of escape. The couple live exclusively for themselves and revel in their resplendent surroundings in a sort of narcissism *à deux*. The purveyors of this myth hold out the promise of a new life to those who can afford to get away from the old one, which is contrasted as pedestrian, humdrum, meaningless.

The myth of island life manipulates our need for wholeness. While creating the illusion of wholeness in the form of love amid natural beauty, it obscures most of reality and of course any form of politics. The apolitical dream is misguided because it subverts love's striving for oneness with all that lives. Dreaming the wrong dream, we try to isolate love from the rest of our world, the world from which we long to escape. Love becomes the prize and the recompense for all the losses and injuries that life has inflicted on us. But love is not compensation for something else. It is not a shield that protects us from disturbances. On the contrary, genuine love melts our defenses and makes us more disturbable. The ecstasy we experience in love heightens our awareness of the violence that imprisons other people and denies them life's fullness. Because we learn to trust through love, which also means unlearning our inclination to distrust, we perceive the unconsoled loneliness, fear, and self-hate right next to us. Because we grow into wholeness through love, we yearn for reconciliation with the disenfranchised of the earth.

In other words, the more I make love, the more I want to make the revolution.

Love is not separable from justice. The drive to make love and to make justice should be one; it will become one the more we overcome the current split between private and public life. As children do not separate parts of their bodies into private, erotic zones and public, desensitized ones, so we may learn not to divide up human sentience into private emotions that we share only with intimates and public, rational modes of exchange that often desensitize us to human need. A scene from Bertolt Brecht's drama *The Caucasian Chalk Circle* will illustrate my point. The kitchen maid Grusha Vashadze, the play's heroine, is forced to flee along with the other inhabitants of the provincial governor's palace because of an enemy invasion. In the turmoil that ensues, the governor's wife deserts her baby son. Grusha finds the infant and hesitates to abandon him despite the dire warnings of her co-workers that anyone found with the governor's heir will be slaughtered by the "Ironshirts." Indecision immobilizes her until something happens, which the narrator recounts:

> As she was standing between courtyard and gate,
> She heard or she thought she heard a low voice calling.
> The child called to her,
> Not whining, but calling quite sensibly,
> Or so it seemed to her.
> "Woman," it said, "help me."
> And it went on, not whining, but saying quite sensibly:
> "Know, woman, he who hears not a cry for help
> But passes by with troubled ears will never hear
> The gentle call of a lover nor the blackbird at dawn
> Nor the happy sigh of the tired grape-picker as the Angelus rings."[5]

Brecht makes it clear that we cannot restrict our emotions to a few people while otherwise hiding and suppressing them. What he calls "the seductive power of goodness"[6] is not selective.

When we close our ears to the cries of the helpless, we kill not only the agape in us but the eros as well. Likewise, we cannot confine love's ecstasy to the private realm without detracting from our public life. The depth of our loving relatedness is decisive for our public life. The fact that First World peoples devote the majority of their natural, intellectual, and financial resources to preparation for war and death is not unrelated to our psychosexual reality. The growth in atomic weaponry tells us something about our capacity for love. If we publicly worship death, how strong then is the personal option for life affirmed in our sexual relationships? What can be said of our emotional vigor if it does not break into politics? In lovemaking we accept our createdness, we re-create and embody ouselves. But if our embodiment in lovemaking does not move us beyond the acute, narrow joys and sorrows of our own bodies to the body politic, then it has not gone far enough.

Earlier I criticized what is called "casual" sex because it does not enable us to grow into wholeness. In a way, however, all our sex is casual, because our lovemaking has not led us to make justice in the world, it has not led us to transform erotic power into revolutionary power. Our intimate personal relationships reach fruition when they connect us to the struggles and sufferings of other people. Transcendence in sexuality leads to solidarity, and the absence of solidarity with others is a sign of the absence of sexual-relatedness. Solidarity intensifies our ecstasy, strengthens our trust, and is essential to our wholeness.

Paul's famous discourse in praise of agape in 1 Corinthians 13 is perhaps the finest biblical expression of the meaning of love. Yet it is astonishing how the traditional reading of Paul's text has managed to circumvent the apostle's wholistic definition of love. A fresh look at Paul's text will reveal that the dimensions of ecstasy, trust, wholeness, and solidarity are present and interconnected in his conception of love.

In 1 Cor. 13:1–3 Paul addresses what we call wholeness. Apart from love, he exhorts, our capacities for religious ecstasy (v. 1), philosophical knowledge and prophetic wisdom (v. 2), and social involvement and charity (v. 3) are nothing. Without agape, acts of ecstasy, wisdom, and charity remain unintegrated attempts to perform deeds of love; they fail to inspire the essential change of heart that genuine love requires. What then is agape? Paul's description of agape echoes the dimensions of love I have tried to identify in this book:

> Love is patient and kind; love is not jealous or boastful; it is not arrogant or rude. Love does not insist on its own way; it is not irritable or resentful; it does not rejoice at wrong, but rejoices in the right. Love bears all things, believes all things, hopes all things, endures all things. (1 Cor. 13:4–7)

There is the dimension of trust and responsibility for each other and the absence of jealousy and arrogance (v. 4). There is the element of solidarity and the absence of opportunism and bitterness (v. 5). Solidarity in love is also marked by self-transcendence: Love "does not rejoice at wrong, but rejoices in the right" (v. 6). The word *panta*, meaning "all" or "all things," is repeated four times in the final verse of this pericope. It expresses the wholistic relatedness of the loving person to others. Elements of agape surface in any wholistic sexual relationship. Instead of subjecting ourselves to the merciless principle of sexual performance, we can learn in our relationships how much comfort human beings can provide for each other. To receive bodily consolation from our partner after undergoing a loss or a trauma is an experience that proves how wrong it is to split off eros from agape. Love indeed bears, believes, hopes, and endures all things (1 Cor. 13:7). Love relates us to the world and makes us sisterly. We become more and more available to each other in a relationship that incorporates both eros and agape. Vivid and unusual testimony to the inseparability of these dimensions of love in the Christian tradition is found in the life of Francis of Assisi, a saint whose spirituality merged eros and agape. Calling himself a "troubadour of God," Francis venerated his beloved Lady Poverty in the form of courtly love songs. His life style exemplified the same mixture of erotic and caring forms of love. There was passion for God and an undivided love for all life in his prayers, sayings, and sometimes foolish deeds. He embraced and kissed the lepers. The community of brothers he lived with created a climate of tenderness and eroticism. They gave away all property and goods given to them. At the same time, they were attuned to the needs of one another, and they repeatedly broke the strict rules of asceticism. Extreme forms of expressing both joy and grief were quite natural to Francis and his followers.

From such a perspective, a life free from passion, extreme vulnerability, and joy is seen as death. In love we gain the certainty of being needed and not simply the awareness of our own needs. Insofar as we are not needed and are replaceable, we are dead. To quote 1 John 3:14, "We know that we have passed out of death into life, because we love the brethren. He who does not love abides in death." The biblical tradition grounds the need to be needed in creation itself. Our reflection on our need for love—for giving and receiving love—reaches a point where it becomes necessary to talk about God as the one who needs us, all of us, unconditionally. God needs our growing capacity to love to continue creation. In the sociopolitical struggle against death, which rules in hunger, exploitation, and war, God will make use of all our passions and our undivided love for life.

NOTES

1. Sex-Pol (sex-political) was an organization founded by Wilhelm Reich in 1932 under the aegis of the German Communist party. A year later the party dissolved the organization and expelled Reich from its membership. Reich defined "orgastic potency" as "the capacity for complete surrender to the flow of biological energy without any inhibition, the capacity for complete discharge of all damned-up sexual excitation." See Wilhelm Reich, *The Function of the Orgasm*, trans. T. P. Wolfe (New York: New World, 1961), p. 79.

2. Albert Ellis, *Sex and the Single Man* (Secaucus, N.J., 1963), p. 56, as quoted in Sam Keen, *The Passionate Life: Stages of Loving* (New York: Harper & Row, 1983), p. 115.

3. Walther Benjamin, *Goethes Wahlverwandschaffen* (Frankfurt, Schriften, Bd. 1, 1955), p. 140.

4. Dorothy Dinnerstein, *The Mermaid and the Minotaur: Sexual Arrangements and Human Malaise* (New York: Harper & Row, 1976), p. 38.

5. Bertolt Brecht, *The Caucasian Chalk Circle* in *Two Plays by Bertolt Brecht*, rev. Eng. versions by Eric Bentley (New York and Scarborough, Ont.: New American Library, 1983), p. 146.

6. Ibid.

13

Created for hope

This book is an attempt to affirm our being created and becoming creators, being liberated and becoming agents of liberation, being loved and becoming lovers. Yet we live in a time when the affirmative power of trusting in the creator is overshadowed again and again by doubt and even despair arising from a unique historical situation in which the global superpowers thwart any regional striving for justice and freedom, while escalating their apocalyptic threat to the whole of creation. Since I began this book, two shattering political events have occurred (both in the fall of 1983) which I sense are endangering not only my life but my faith as well. The first catastrophic event was the deployment of new first-strike nuclear weapons in Western Europe, a development rejected by 78 percent of the population of West Germany and yet imposed upon them. Having been personally involved in the great movement for peace since its revival in December 1979, I now find myself, together with millions of other Europeans, at an impasse, faced with what seem to be the only choices left: resignation or violence. After four years of nonviolent struggle against implacable, media-manipulated political propaganda alleging the necessity of nuclearization, the remaining options appear to be to give up or to go crazy, to resign ourselves to the fact that West Germany is an occupied country, or to fight the policy of the warmongers with the desperate means of war. We ask ourselves, Is there a third way, something other than resignation and losing our souls or civil war and losing our lives? Where is hope? The bomb is killing me insofar as it destroys my capacity to trust in creation and its continuity in history.

The second ominous political event was the invasion of Grenada by U.S. troops, an event seen by many as a warm-up exercise for an invasion of Nicaragua. Because I visited Nicaragua in August 1983 and learned more about the Sandinista's unique revolution (their first legal act was to ban the death penalty), I feel personally crushed by the envisioned scenario of a blood bath that would annihilate those whose only crime is calling for more justice. Under the threat of these two events, my question is not so much the old Leninist question, What is to be done? My question is a more elementary one: Where is there any hope for the powerless? And this question leads me to another: How can we possibly praise the creative power of life and celebrate our having been created for love and justice in light of these events and their future implications?

This is a time when I sense that my own hope, as well as the secular hope for a decent, reasonable government, is too feeble. We need more encouragement than we are able to extract from our present situation. As a Christian, I stand in a long tradition that is not at all equivocal. It is a tradition of failure more than hope, of defeat more than victory. And yet it has its own enduring claims on life, and our being created in the image of God is one of its strongest claims. For me, the advantage of being a part of a religious tradition is that I am both obliged and allowed to listen to the voices of the mothers and fathers in my tradition. They too faced defeat and isolation and found themselves overpowered by the mightiest powers of this world. They too saw their hopes trampled by their own war-lusty people. They too saw their own nations put their faith in wealth and military violence instead of in God's justice. But looking back on the Christian legacy, I am also aware of other, momentous experiences that push back the defeat, that invalidate the violence. The tradition tells stories of an exodus from a military superpower and the resurrection of life from death by execution, so it sustains and clarifies my faith. My forebears help me to ground my hope in the power of life which they called God.

I am reminded specifically of three "church fathers" who have purged my hope of illusions and rescued it from despair: Paul, Augustine, and Karl Marx. In the classical New Testament passage on hope in Romans 4, Paul talks about Abraham as the father of the nations. Abraham believed in God and cleaved to God's promises: "In hope he believed against hope" (Rom. 4:18). The concept of hope is instrumental in Paul's discussion of justification by faith versus justification by law. He locates hope in this dialectic. For Paul, hope does not spring from our deeds or intentions; it precedes them. To the majority of secular philosophers in Paul's time, hope was regarded not as a virtue but as a weakness, a weakness attributed to women. Hope was considered "a temporary illusion for the unwise." Paul gives an accurate description of these people when he says that the pagans have no hope (Eph. 2:12; 1 Thess. 4:13), for the pagans are those who have no hope, whatever their religion.

Paul's major dispute was with Jewish law. Paul sees the law as a dead, frozen, oppressive structure, not as a serious expression of one's religious belief in justification. Instead of being "the way," which is the original Jewish understanding of the torah, the law, according to Paul, is a sterile and empty system of rules that functions as a virtual barrier between God and God's people. It is not my purpose here to explore all the facets and ramifications of Paul's controversy with Judaism, but I do want to state that Paul's polemic against the Jewish law seems to be a productive misunderstanding of the authentic meaning of torah. What Paul calls faith as opposed to law correlates with the authentic Jewish understanding that lies at the heart of the torah. What he calls law we would call in modern terms an ideology with strict rules of conduct.

To the Protestant Reformation leader Martin Luther, Paul's law was comparable to the Catholicism of Luther's time, a belief system of normative rules that eclipsed God. God was hidden behind the law and secreted especially from the illiterate masses. It was obvious to both Paul and Luther that the law held out no hope for the hopeless. The law was a demanding and rewarding system for a certain caste of people, the lay and religious elite, which excluded the vast majority and made God inaccessible to them. The inaccessibility of God or truth is the mainstay of law in the ideological sense of the word as Paul uses it. This God does not offer hope to the outcast, nor in the long run to anyone.

Is there anything comparable in our times, something we would call "law"? Today we need to identify our law, which is no longer a religious code. We need to examine the ideological structure that controls our lives, demands and rewards our unquestioned obedience, and robs us of hope. In Paul's religious debate with Judaism, the law precluded

X the possibility of God's spontaneity and grace; there was no hope for those who failed to observe it. Today we might identify science as the universally acknowledged belief system in our world that demands and rewards our acceptance of its premises and goals at the price of our hope. Science, seemingly a neutral and value-free system of cognition, has become a law as restrictive and repressive for dissenters as the Jewish law was in Paul's time. The ideology of science is a belief system that binds and rewards its priests and makes hope into a prescientific, unnecessary relic, because there is no space for hope and unpredictability inside its rationally controlled system. If, for the purpose of reflection, we replace the word "science" for Paul's word "law," we may read Paul's text on hope as follows:

> The promise to Abraham and his descendants, that they should inherit the world, did not come through *science* but through the righteousness of faith. If it is the adherents of *science* who are to be the heirs, faith is null and the promise is void. . . . That is why it depends on faith, in order that the promise may rest on grace and be guaranteed to all his descendants—not only to the adherents of *science* but also to those who share the faith of Abraham, for he is the father of us all, as it is written, "I have made you the father·of many nations"—in the presence of the God in whom he believed, who gives life to the dead and calls into existence the things that do not exist. In hope he believed against hope, that he should become the father of many nations. (Rom. 4:13–18a)

Or we might insert another ideological "law" of our times, namely, anticommunism, the ideology that insists that all evil comes from communism. Then we would read that the promise is given to Abraham's descendants not through anticommunism but through faith.

Faith needs hope which is not an irrelevancy or an illusion. Hope is life's response to life's call. Hope goes against the prolongation of what is given. *Spes contra spem*, hope against hope, means transcendence of
⊁ the given. Hope does not depend for its existence on what a person may be able to do for herself; it is inseparable from faith in a transcendent power that some call God. And the kind of faith that I am talking about does not necessarily have anything to do with the trappings of institutionalized religion. Those who claim to believe in God but have no hope for the survival of humankind, who further or tolerate the preparation for Armageddon, truly do not beleive in God. A God-ideology

without hope is not faith. But those who have hope and share it through their lives and deeds truly believe in God whether or not they use religious language and talk about "faith" and "God."

Augustine is another "church father" who made me understand the role of hope. In a remarkable deviation from the teaching of Paul, who contends in 1 Cor. 13:13 that of the virtues of faith, hope, and love, love is the greatest, Augustine maintains that of these three theological virtues hope is the greatest. According to Augustine, faith only tells us that God is, and love only tells us that God is good, but hope tells us that God will work God's will. From my perspective, God's will is justice for all. But how does God work God's will? How does she do that? Where? With whom? Who are her allies and her co-workers? These are the most important questions for anyone who wants to work in the church today. And as we grapple with these questions it is helpful to remember another Augustinian insight that Hope has two lovely daughters, Anger and Courage—anger so that what cannot be, may not be, and courage so that what must be, will be.

There is finally a third "church father" who sustains my hope against hope—Karl Marx. One of the most important things I have learned from Marx is that any socio-economic analysis that neither uncovers the contradictions nor identifies the agents of change in a given historical situation is both superficial and deleterious. It is not enough simply to describe what is without consideration for what is yet to be, without regard for the sources of hope. I think that struggle is the source of hope. There is no hope without struggle. There is no hope that drops from heaven through the intervention of God. Hope lies within the struggle. An analysis that is nothing but an analysis serves the maintenance of the status quo. It is not enough to delineate things in a scientific way if that will not change reality. We must work toward the time when the inner contradictions of a system of social injustice become so obvious that they move people from apathy to struggle, from despair to hope. A good analysis has to identify the victims of injustice in a particular social context and ask, How long will they tolerate it? How long will they keep silent? When will they fight back? Who are the bearers of change? What are the objective conditions of struggle and therefore of hope?

Hope lies with those oppressed people who cease tolerating oppression and move to struggle against it. There is no other hope than with those who fight, those who feel oppressed enough and empowered enough to fight to exorcise the oppressor from our midst. There is an apt phrase in German: *Wer sich nicht wehrt, lebt verkehrt*—He or she who doesn't fight back lives wrongly. From a religious standpoint, the person who does not fight back lives wrongly toward God. Those who do not fight back do not believe in love or hope. In my opinion, a group of Christians who call themselves a church are a church only if they fight back. To live in resistance is what is meant by hope against hope.

With a view to resistance, I would like to reflect once more on the concept of creation. Is there an interrelation between faith in creation and our becoming resisters? How might we finally bring together the biblical traditions of creation and liberation? The connectedness of the two concepts becomes visible when we rid ourselves of an exclusively past-oriented understanding of creation and fully accept that creation is unfinished, that it continues.

We may distinguish three biblically based forms of creation. The first creation that brought us into being is visualized in Genesis 1. In contemplating this text, I have always found a certain consolation in the knowledge that the winds, the waters, the earth, the air, the fish, and the birds were there before we humans were called into being. Being, as it is depicted in Genesis, means being-in-relation, living in togetherness. When I think about death, and that means contemplating my own death, I feel part of this planet called earth. When I pass away, the winds and the waters, the earth and the air, the fish and the birds, and all the other animals will continue to exist. Why then should I fear death? It is because of the interrelatedness of the created universe that Francis of Assisi was able to speak about death as "our sister." To talk this way is the greatest affirmation of creation we can make, for it means that we have integrated death into life. Then we are able to see our little beings as part of the great Being to which we will return, sister to Sister Death, child to Mother Earth, brother to Brother Sun, drop to the great Waters, flame to the Light.

I am afraid, however, that human beings today are a part of nonbeing, that our unrelatedness is catapulting us into undoing creation and all that lives on the small planet earth. I fear that nothingness will supersede being, that the bomb is in our hearts as well as in our hands, and that we hate creation because we have chosen to live under the bomb. No generation in history was ever able to say no to creation as we can. No generation has heretofore been able to kill not just Jesus Christ again and again but God the creator, the Being-in-relation. We may fool ourselves with superficial Christian slogans about the "Eternal God," but there will not be any heavenly father or mother or creator after the nuclear holocaust, after the final solution.

Traditional Christians sometimes misconstrue the concept of creation in a fatalistic way. And those on the far right are prone to manipulate this sensibility, claiming that God is in charge of everything and that should he decide to undo his creation no love of mothers for their children, no rational behavior on the part of reasonable beings, no resistance against the strategies of death will stop him. Political leaders who appropriate this theology and talk seriously about Armageddon disclose their secret lust for power over life and death and pave the way for military planners who account for megadeaths in their war scenarios.

This pseudo-religious ideology is heresy, disguised as pious surrender to the will of God. It mixes up God and Satan until they are indistinguishable. Is it Satan who wants to terminate creation, or is it God? To the purveyors of military fascism, it hardly matters; for them, the unifying concept that counts is power. Power is worthy of adoration, nothing else. And it is power that triumphs when right-wing Christians subordinate themselves to the "princes of this world" in a seemingly devout surrender to the will of an ill-defined God. The power of those who command the military-industrial complex, who steer us toward death, is kept intact by Christians who cry out "His will, not ours" as they embrace the nuclear option. Theirs is a religious ideology in which an authoritarian God enters into a nightmarish alliance with the unconscious wish to eradicate the cities of the enemy or, in the Pentagon's own language, to decapitate their leaders as one decapitates a chicken. In this ideology God does not live where justice and love bloom; God reigns as the supreme superpower. In this ideology the concept of creation is severed from notions of love and justice and is thus transformed into an expression of the absolute right of the superpower to do what it wants with its subjects.

If we want to respond to creation differently, with loving care for all that lives on the earth, and if we aspire to become what we were meant to be, that is, co-creators, created in God's image, then we must realize that creation refers not only to our origin but to our future as well. The creation that began with the first creation is unfinished.

The second creation that brought us into being is revealed in the Exodus story as the time when the people of God passed through the Red Sea out of slavery and into the land of freedom. The second creation happens in history. There is a great exodus in progress today out of the Egypt of militarism and dependency into a land where peace and justice may embrace each other. To remember our second creation in history, our flight from Egypt and the slave house, is to think about all the peoples, such as the El Salvadorans, who are currently struggling to make their long and painful way out of the Egypt of their oppressors. The second creation is also not yet finished. Each generation must define its understanding of freedom in a new way. Today the people of Europe offer a new definition of freedom: Freedom means freedom from nuclear weapons; life means living without bombs, and we will not be free as long as we live with them.

There is a third creation that the Bible talks about symbolically as our baptism into death and rebirth in Jesus Christ. The "new woman" and the "new man" come into being in a process of death and resurrection:

> Do you not know that all of us who have been baptized into Christ Jesus were baptized into his death? We were buried therefore with him by baptism into death, so that as Christ was raised from the dead by the glory of the Father, we too might walk in the newness of life. For if we have been united with him in a death like his, we shall certainly be united with him in a resurrection like his. We know that our old self was crucified with him so that . . .we might no longer be enslaved to sin. (Rom. 6:3–6)

To be reborn we have to die with Christ, which means that the old self is crucified with Christ. Who is the "old man" or the "old woman" who has to die? It is the old being: the egotistic, the self-concerned, the apolitical human being. It is often the pious self caught up in a form of spirituality that glorifies individualism. But the sinful self referred to by the apostle Paul may just as easily be the secular individualist who affirms the decency and goodness of his own life while blinding himself to the scope of concrete suffering in our world.

The "old being" who must die is not only the egocentric; she is also the powerless human being who feels incapable of changing anything in her world. She is, as Paul puts it, "enslaved to sin." She is a slave to the powers who prepare the nuclear holocaust, a slave to injustice and the destruction of the earth. Egotism and powerlessness are the main characteristics of the old being.

The new human being is born in the resurrection of Christ. He and she are empowered to fight death and those who hold us under the sway of death. The new human being in Christ is a resister, a revolutionary. She knows that for which she lives and gives her life. He is a fighter for the city of God. The new human being is a loving being who participates in the three forms of creation as a co-creator. He and she are committed to the renewal of the earth, to our liberation from bondage, and to resistance against death and all the powers of death. The third creation is as unfinished as the other two. All three creations continue still.

We cannot afford to have a naive trust in the first creation. The "fate of the earth" in a nuclear age, which Jonathan Schell has illuminated so well for us in a book by that name, is not something about which we may rest assured because it lies in God's hands. The fate of the earth is equally in our hands, and only a community of resisters may prevent the extermination of humankind and the rest of creation. The God who created the universe, including our planet, and who delivered us from slavery is the same God who raises the dead to new life, so that we who were dead and without hope might become resisters and lovers of life. "Lover of the living" is an old name for God (Wis. of Sol. 11:26). So shall it be our name for evermore.